LIVING TOGETHER

Andrea Riccardi

Living Together

New City

London

First published in Great Britain by
New City
Unit 17, Sovereign Park
Coronation Road,
London NW10 7QP
©2008 New City, London

Cover Design by Tomeu Mayans
Picture back cover: © Domenico Salmaso

British Cataloguing in Publication Data:
A catalogue reference for this book is available from the British Library

ISBN 978-1-905039-04-3

Typeset by New City
Printed and bound in Great Britain by Cromwell Press, Trowbrige, Wilstshire

CONTENTS

5

CAN WE LIVE TOGETHER?

A question from Rwanda

In Kigali, capital of Rwanda, I visited the Genocide Memorial, called the Kigali Memorial Centre. It was Easter, 2005. Little more than ten years had passed since those tragic events. The memory of them was still very vivid. The prisons were still heaving with people on trial for crimes to do with genocide. You could identify those found guilty by their pink clothing they wore as they went to work. Problems from the genocide were still impending. The settled policy aim of President Kagame is that those terrible events will never be repeated. He led the armed struggle that overthrew the Hutu regime in Kigali and put an end to the massacre of the Tutsis. For the President, Hutus and Tutsis do not exist, but only those guilty of genocide and its victims. Power, wielded by him, a Tutsi, guarantees the veracity of the numbers of those who were victims of the genocide.

However, the people continue to think in terms of Hutu and Tutsi. How and when full democracy will become a reality remains an open question. Will Tutsis and Hutus ever be able to live together peacefully?

The Kigali Memorial Centre is the monument to this terrible memory: one sees the coffins of those assassinated, whilst a sequence of images guides the visitor to the focal point, a room carpeted with skulls. The message is clear: deep horror at what happened in 1994. And a question arises: "How was it possible for next-door neighbours to have murdered people whom they had always known?" The killers did not come from far away, they were people who had always lived near to their victims. In a beautiful yet tragic book *With Machete Blows*, Jean Hatzfeld has described the perpetrators of the genocide. They do not seem to be monsters; often they are normal people who have been transformed by the influence of propaganda and a collective conformist madness. The killers were convinced they could no longer live with the Tutsis who were a constant threat for the Hutus. Therefore they had to be eliminated.

The images in the Kigali Memorial Centre show the fear born of living with people who became murderers. Yet the Tutsis are no different from the Hutus, not even in language. As at Yad Vashem, the Holocaust memorial in Jerusalem, so too in Kigali, it is the stories of the children that touch one most. We are told about the favourite food of Francine Murenzi Ingabire, a twelve-year-old: it is fried eggs, and her favourite sport is swimming, adding that she was killed with a machete. Their whole life has been stolen from these children. Why? So as to protect other children?

As we are painfully led through the rooms and down the corridors of the Memorial, the ever-present question is this, "How will Hutus and Tutsis ever be able to live together in peace after all this has happened?" Kagame, with his policies, is trying to map out a way, despite doubts in international public opinion, which is critical of the heavy methods being used. And, ten years after the genocide, the outlook is still thick with disquiet, precisely because of the "mixed" composition of the Rwandan population and its dramatic history.

Rwandans are not differentiated ethnically by a language, but by history, by old and recent discriminations and by social activities. There is a ditch between them, or rather an abyss, caused by the genocide of 1994. Will they be able to live together in the Rwanda of tomorrow? This question applies

8

not only to Rwanda but also to Burundi which has a similar ethnic make-up – Hutu and Tutsi – and a very difficult history weighing it down. In Burundi, they have chosen to follow a different road, with its new Hutu president and a system of checks and balances between the two ethnic groups.

The case of Rwanda is not an isolated one in the region. The problem is general. It presents itself in other forms in several countries of Africa and maybe throughout the rest of the world too. The Rwandans wanted to locate their own genocide in the context of a long, sad gallery of similar events elsewhere. We can see this at the Kigali Memorial Centre. There is a haunting sequence of cross-references and images of genocide in the twentieth century. There is the slaughter of the African population of Hereros by the Germans in Namibia (65,000 killed between 1904 and 1905), the massacre of the Armenians, the Holocaust, the Cambodian genocide, and the Balkans in the 1990s – very different situations, yet all revealing the cruel side of the past century.

As I left the Kigali Memorial, I kept asking myself: "How can we live together, when there are so many dangerous situations in our world?" These are questions to do with Rwanda and Burundi, but not about them alone. These questions confront me with more and more of the difficult situations in Africa. Differing ethnic, linguistic or religious communities are intermixed in Africa and they live in the same country, whose boundaries were arbitrarily laid down by colonizers without regard to any ethnic realities.

How to live together is the problem for Christians and Muslims in that huge African country of Nigeria. The first great African crisis after de-colonization was the terrible war for the independence of Biafra from 1967-1970. The image of the skeletal Biafran child came to typify the misery of Africa. But there were so many other crises in the final decades of the century. How to live together is the problem of the Ivory

Coast, a country divided to this day into North and South, Muslim and Christian areas, and with uncertainty as to the identity of the immigrant part of its population. There is the question of the small but significant Togo, run by a political group which is identical with an ethnic minority of little over 10%, the heirs of the late President Eyadema. The country is demanding equality in human rights.

There is no shortage of examples. To live together within the framework of one state is a big problem for Africa, above all because the institutions of the state are weak. That is the harsh story for so many independent nations.

But this question is not only to do with Africa, a consequence of conditions in that particular continent. We find the same in Asia, starting from Sri Lanka – overrun for decades by a terrible guerrilla war – through to Indonesia, struggling with separatists in its Aceh region. This is the history of so many minorities who demand their space, their autonomy, and even their independence. This is the predicament of the so-called indigenous populations in Guatemala, Bolivia, Peru and Ecuador. It is often the history of diverse, overlapping communities that find themselves in the same territories or in the same cities. The fury against the Chinese minority, who have an economic hegemony in Indonesia, reveals a serious accumulation of tension in Asian society. Amy Chua, a Chinese scholar at Yale University in the United States, starting from the experience of her own dispersed family, has pointed out the risk of a growth in hostility towards economic minorities that are strong in societies which now understand processes of democratization and liberation. The less wealthy majority proclaim themselves as the legitimate "proprietors" of the well-being of the country and pitch themselves against the rich minority. This is happening against the English colonials in Mugabe's Zimbabwe, but it is also present among the indigenous peoples in the Philippines or Bolivia.

A question which concerns us

Living together amid diversity is not just a problem for the peripheral areas of the world, such as nascent democracies, states without freedom or states with arbitrarily drawn boundaries. It is also a European question. Think of the Balkans. The wars in former Yugoslavia, those in Bosnia-Herzegovina, have posed the problem of living together for the Bosnian Muslims, Serbian Orthodox, and Croatian Catholics. This is a story which has turned out well with ethnic separation, after the spilling of so much blood and so much accumulated hatred. I have followed closely the events in Kosovo, lived in by an Albanian majority and a Serb minority, under the rule of the government in Belgrade. Despite the country's present autonomy, the problem is still unresolved. The Serb villages are still surrounded by the Albanian population and protected by international troops. Life is impossible for the Serb minority. Moreover, all the events of the 1990s in the former Yugoslavia tell a story of a painful break-up of the structure of living together which had been set up by Tito. He was dealing with a partly artificial reality created with the ending of the Hapsburg Empire. Its fall signalled a declaration of the impossibility of living together with others on the part of the Slav peoples in the south (that is to say the Yugoslavs). This happened after the fall of the Berlin wall, whilst Europe was enforcing its process of unification.

Today, living together is a manifest, explicit problem, even in the most solid of the European nations. For a long time, the problem has been located in the awakening of minorities, from the Basques in Spain to the people of Northern Ireland. Meanwhile Flemings and Walloons in Belgium are eroding more and more of the structures of a unitary state in a small country which is important in the history of the nineteenth and twentieth centuries only because of its extensive colonial

11

territories in the Congo, Rwanda and Burundi. However, the most serious problem is to do with the communities of non-European immigrants. This is the problem of the peripheral, the marginal zones of European cities. It exploded recently in a series of conflicts in the suburbs of Paris and other French cities, with the revolt of the younger generation, who were often the children of immigrants.

The revolt by these young people – mostly African and Moorish in origin, but largely second or even third generation French – seems to have been a primitive "collision of civilizations". On one side is France, with its national symbols, and on the other is this rebellious reaction. The young people are isolated and have no jobs and no hope. In some ways, the revolt fits into a tradition of rebellion which is a feature of the history of France. On the other hand, it cannot be explained solely by Islam. These young people are demonstrating against exclusion and inequality in a rudimentary language, violence. The tensions are not new, nor are the acts of violence unpublicized, but at the present time they are breaking out simultaneously in different places. Rebellion is gaining strength and developing with the globalization of information. The short-circuit of television publicity has given the young people an identity, "We are famous, even CNN talks about us," a young rebel said to me in November 2005. Another declared in a newspaper, "We are prepared to sacrifice everything, because we have nothing." In four days, from 5 to 8 November, almost 3000 cars were burned in the Paris region. This was their way of affirming their identity and their presence on the French scene. "I burn, therefore I am."

What is behind these people? In the first place, there are the great voids in the suburbs: crises in social and educational networks and in the relationships between institutions and people. There is also the ending of the Communist party and its roots in society; this used to transfer much of the social pressure on to the field of political confrontation. There is the crisis in the parishes of French Catholicism, which in the post-war period addressed the problem of the "red suburbs". And there is the crisis in family life, even if one asserts that immigrant families are different from European ones. This is a common problem for all of the West, which is seeing its families disintegrate, and this means that men and women grow up alone, without an education in the realities of common life – which is the family – in which differences of sex, age, generation and ability, all live together in unity and with a sense of a common destiny.

The rebellious children of the suburbs are creating an elementary identity for themselves in reaction to their marginalization in a society where the pressure of inequality is being ever more deeply felt. It is the revolt of the young against the "old" society. The inter-ethnic nature of the gangs is the fruit of exclusion, therefore the greater part of the young people are from immigrant families. They are using violence to draw attention to themselves. They are not asking for negotiations. This is a revolt, a deep dissension that we must decode. The young are feeling that they are the dregs of the city and of the world of work. This France is not their France. How can they be integrated and their aspirations engaged with? Are we finding ourselves faced with the rebellion of the immigrants against the state belonging to the majority of the people?

The question of the indigenous majority and the immigrants living together is often presented in an aggressive and populist manner, whereas it would be better to reflect on it calmly and realistically.

The attacks in London in July 2005 had set off an alarm signal. The fact that the terrorists might be British citizens (Muslim by religion and Pakistani in origin) has shed light on an issue which has been around for years, and which became insistent after 9/11. How can Europeans of ancient origin live in peace and security with the new immigrants, especially the Muslims? Can Islamic communities be integrated? Are they not hiding terrible potential enemies in their midst? Did we not see the young attackers in London with their British passports and belonging to families well embedded into society? Well then, how is it still possible to live together, and, what is more, let these minorities be reinforced by new waves of migrants? These are questions regarding the large Muslim communities in Great Britain, France and Germany, and also in Holland and Belgium. Some people loudly denounce European Islam as the fifth column of Islamic expansion in Europe. The great Polish traveller-novelist Ryszard Kapuscinski has observed that the integration of Islam "is one of the most fascinating pieces of enquiry that Europe is called upon to face." Perhaps this is the greatest question facing the Europe of tomorrow.

So then, the question is to do with the whole of immigration (which, nevertheless, is an economic and social necessity in a continent with a falling population). Is not the immigrant community changing the character and the identity of Europe? The British choice, to allow the development of such communities without imposing any special regime of integration on them (unlike, for example, France) has been called into question by the events in London in July 2005. But if Great Britain is weeping, France is certainly not smiling about the revolts in its suburban areas.

The question of living together assumes different features from region to region, but is a crucial question for national institutions, and for religions, politics and relations between races. Is it possible to live together when we are so different? This question comes woven into others that are equally important, "What do the differences really tell us?" "What is the threshold below which differences are compatible?"

In the 1950s, during my childhood as a boy from Rome in a primary school in Northern Italy, I used to hear the barbed remarks aimed at the southern Italians who had moved to those regions. They were often rather disdainfully called "Moroccans". I heard about the North which was working and the South which was eating. Today, I smile at the very thought of those frictions between northern and southern Italians, even if the Northern League seems to have re-launched them.

The problems of today are very different and more dramatic, whilst the idea of a multicultural society creaks and groans. Every period in history has its own perception of the threshold of how much diversity is compatible within itself. In France, faced with emigration between the two wars (Italian, Armenian, Polish, East European), people were predicting a crisis for French identity. There was no crisis, but in history nothing repeats itself. Today we have a perception which is very preoccupied with the threshold of compatibility and about living together in diversity. Terrorism, which is staining the cities of Europe with blood, makes this perception all the more intense.

Faced with differing situations at every level, the question keeps repeating, "How are we to live together?" Politicians and intellectuals ask it, but so do ordinary men and women who also watch daily events and find they have no solution to the problems, nor do they have any ideals concerning society. The reality is that, while we are considering this question, we are already living together in many areas. It is happening in Western Europe, where the large cities have taken on a multi-religious and multi-ethnic appearance, while still keeping their traditional Western-Christian framework and their secular organisations. It is happening in so many parts of the world. Apart from cohabiting with each other as a result of physical and geographical proximity, a virtual living together is becoming a reality, through which the life, culture and tastes of one area of the human race are joining up with those of others via the channels of globalization. Traditions and flavours are mixing together in the global community. Travel takes people to other countries. Emigration creates deep bonds. The mobility of people, their ideas and their customs knows no boundaries. Living together seems an inevitable destiny. But this is not always reassuring.

"Is it possible to live together?" Alain Tourain, an astute French observer of contemporary society, asks this in the subtitle of his demanding book *Liberty, Equality, Diversity.* This is the question that I wish to address in the following pages: "How can we live together?" I am aware that there is no single answer. One must endeavour to find different answers for diverse situations, cultures and countries. The answer that we hear repeated with growing insistence – especially in moments of crisis or when faced with sudden flare-ups – is that we must reinforce frontiers and create a bigger defensive wall. But fear is not the answer, nor are fine sentiments. Contemporary life is inevitably bringing us – as the saying goes – "to live as neighbours amidst diversity". It is normal for similar questions to arise to which there is no immediate answer, yet it may be necessary to try to address them patiently.

CHAPTER 1

STORIES OF DIVORCE BETWEEN NATIONS

The nation: a homogeneous extended family

During the twentieth century, there was much grief in places where different nations were in cohabitation. These "divorces" frequently took place through grave crises, violence, displacement of populations and massacres. A territory would believe itself to be in a secure and "natural" condition only when its population was as homogeneous as possible; that, at least, was the prevailing opinion or aspiration. Common language, ethnicity, culture, religion and history (sometimes plus epic poems) were the foundation of this national homogeneity which underpinned the state. Admittedly, even in the heart of Europe, there were some high-profile exceptions, such as Switzerland which is both multi-national and multi-religious.

The spectre that troubled the sleep of rulers in the nineteenth century – especially the rulers of the three great empires, the Hapsburg, the Ottoman, and the Russian – was the nation, not the proletariat. So what is a nation? In an important lecture at the Sorbonne in 1882, Ernest Renan, author of the celebrated *Life of Jesus*, an intellectual loaded with honours by the Third Republic, gave this answer, "So then, the nation is one great solidarity, constructed around awareness of sacrifices achieved and by those sacrifices which people are still disposed to achieve together." And he added with emphasis, "the existence of a nation (forgive the metaphor) is like a daily referendum." Voluntarism, policy, consensus – the daily "referendum" –

were the crucial elements when considering a nation. And such they remain. An eminent Italian historian, Frederico Chabod, insisted that this nationalism belonged to another kind of political genre when compared with the positivism of German nationalism, with its great sensitivity to race and territory.

Whatever form it might take, the nation and nationalism disturbed Europe and the Mediterranean for more than a century. If a nation consists in a willingness to live together, to travel into the future together and to make sacrifices together, it means at the same time a decision to struggle against others, or at least to exclude others from one's own territory. Throughout the nineteenth and twentieth centuries, political affairs redesigned the notion of "We" with incredible speed throughout Europe and the Mediterranean. In different places and in different combinations of elements, the "plebiscite" was to create nations, but, at the same time, it also drew the boundaries of foreignness. This is not a history of nationalism written in a few pages. Suffice it to remember that the development of the idea of a nation which captivates hearts and minds is, in many cases, also stating the ending of a tapestry of cohabitation between peoples and communities, different ethnically and in religion. Unexpectedly, these different communities also began to look at themselves differently because they had been turned into nations.

The era of nations coincides with the ending of so many situations of the inter-religious and multi-ethnic cohabitation which had characterised a significant part of the European and Mediterranean world. What was being affirmed was the reality of nationhood founded upon homogeneity and also upon the marginalization of forms of diversity. It was an ancient model – one can find it in fourth century Spain in the *Limpieza de sangre* and in struggles against Jews and Muslims – a model different from the Catholic tradition by which Muslims and Jews, once converted, were Christian and "blood" counted for nothing.

18

Against this nationalist model there stood a secular, imperial and cosmopolitan experience which had profoundly influenced European and Mediterranean civilization, causing different peoples to live together. The new nations called for homogeneity in language, in territory, in ethnicity, and in religion. This was not easy to fulfil in territories where the history and the deposits of empires had created stratified communities, which were sometimes interwoven. Faced with this reality, nationalism had to produce new and homogeneous situations. To do this, it assimilated, converted or, in extreme cases of resistant identities, expelled others: in the final resort, it exterminated them.

The case of the Balkans

The history of the age of nations is not identical everywhere. It is not cruel everywhere. It meant the death of the empires. On the one hand, the Hapsburg and the Ottoman Empires died with the First World War, and on the other, the Tsarist Empire was radically transformed into the Soviet Union. People could no longer live together (except in the extreme coercion of the USSR). The history of the twentieth century ended with the terrible dismembering of Yugoslavia in the 1990s. Out of that federation were born Slovenia, Croatia (after great contention with the Serbs), Macedonia (with an important Albanian minority), Serbia and Montenegro and Bosnia-Herzegovina which had been administered by Austria since 1878, then annexed by it in 1908, so taking it out of Ottoman sovereignty to become part of Yugoslavia in 1918.

Between 1992 and 1995, Bosnia went through some very painful disasters, stained with massacres, displacement of populations and ethnic cleansing. Living together within the borders of Bosnia there were Serbs (Orthodox), Croatians

(Catholic) and Muslims. This was the inheritance from the old imperial Ottoman ethnic interweaving where populations were mixed together. The Muslim community had been deliberately treated as a nation by Tito, and had even developed its own contacts with Third World Muslim countries, but had not exhibited a strong character and identity in the Communist epoch. However, in the heat of conflict and under heavy pressure, it rapidly found both. Bosnia-Herzegovina was the epicentre of the conflict, the place where the virulent pathology of the impossibility of living together was made glaringly clear. The solution, two centuries old, was separation. This happened in a simpler way for Slovenia; in 1990 it detached itself from Yugoslavia. But how could it be possible to detach oneself when living in the same cities and in the same territories? That was the drama of Bosnia.

This is an old and painful question which arises punctually whenever great empires are dismembered. Yugoslavia was born precisely as a compromise after 1918, when the Austro-Hungarian Empire was broken up and it was thought possible to put together diverse peoples, mainly Slavic, in a small empire around the Serbian monarchy. The Communist hegemony succeeded that of Serbia after the Second World War. The war in Yugoslavia had seen resistance against Italian and German invaders, but there had also been internecine conflict among the Yugoslavs. After the war and following the Fascist occupation, the Italians of Istria and Dalmatia (about 250,000) had to leave lands in which they had lived for centuries. Several thousands lost their lives. After the Italian victory in the First World War, these lands had been annexed by Italy and Italianized, despite being an ethnic amalgam. With its defeat in the Second World War, the Italians were to pay a high price for that policy.

For several decades the problem of nationalism had been shackled by the Yugoslav "monarchy" whether dynastic or communist in nature. This was the "little empire" of the Southern Slavs, which, in the communist epoch, became one of the leading countries in the movement of non-aligned nations. This construction collapsed disastrously beneath the hammer-blows of nationalistic passions, despite an ingenious constitutional system inherited from Tito. With the ending of the communist ideology, various predominant nationalisms arose. There were the better known ones, such as the Croatian and Slovenian, but also the silent ones, like Islam. Above all, one predominant conviction became clear, that it was not possible to live together and that each community had to have its own nation-state. It had been more than a hundred years since the shudder of nationalist passions had been felt in the Balkans and Eastern Europe, often accompanied by massacres and the displacement of populations. Yet nation-states had also been born out of these processes.

Kosovo is the ancient cradle of the Serbian nation and the homeland of her sacred sites, but today it is inhabited by an overwhelming Albanian majority. In 1998 and 1999, the Albanians experienced harsh repression from Milosevic's Serbs, including forced migrations and massacres. It was the final phase in the crisis of Yugoslavia. Today, the remaining Serb minority lives under international control in areas protected by foreign troops. They too have suffered their tragedies, and the Serbian oppressors of yesterday have become a ghettoised minority. There is so much hatred. Jonathan Sacks, a philosopher and theologian who is Chief Rabbi of the British Commonwealth was quite correct to write, "The virus of hatred can seem to have fallen asleep for a time, but it rarely dies." And he added, "Friends become enemies; neighbours become competitors. Then the wall of separation is the lesser evil, but that is often not enough to bring an end to violence." That has been the story of Yugoslavia, neighbours discovering that they cannot live side by side.

The Ottoman inheritance: cohabitation and turmoil

A separating wall becomes the solution when life together becomes hell. No matter if this wall is a physical reality, like the one that the state of Israel has built on its borders with the Palestinian Territories, or if it is a new frontier, or, in extreme cases, it turns out to be the interposing of international armed forces, either provisionally or destined to stay for years.

In Cyprus, a frontier has divided the Greek from the Turkish part for more than thirty years. The agrarian world of the Turks seems years and miles away from the Greek area which is so heavily developed, even if they are two parts of the same island, cut in half by a frontier that has been closed for a long time. The separation came about in 1974 after the failure of the cohabitation regime under President Archbishop Makarios. There had been an ingenious system of checks and balances to allow Greeks and Turks to live together. It was overthrown by the Greek colonels and became unacceptable to the Turks, who were suspicious of Greek aims. Next the Turks reinforced their minority population with emigration from Anatolia. The courageous step of separation seems to have been the most reasonable solution. Maybe it is, sometimes. But often the practical realities make the division very painful, because so many communities and connections are suppressed. The partition of Cyprus caused painful migrations and an unnatural division between two states on one island. But it is only one example of many.

The events in the Balkans are a chapter in the history of the vanished Ottoman empire, which was the heir of the great Arab-Muslim expansion and also of Byzantium, which both experienced and practised the superimposing of populations on to one another. Turks were scattered in all territories under Ottoman control, whilst various population groups were Islamized. Jews used to live everywhere. Cities played host to very diverse communities: in Istanbul there were Greek, Armenian, Turkish, Jewish, Bulgarian, and Far Eastern people. To Jerusalem went Arab Muslims, Arab Christians, and Jews, to Alexandria went Arabs, but also Greeks, Italians, and Jews. The Sublime Portal ruled a multi-national, and multi-religious world. The nation-states which succeeded the Ottoman Empire gave accounts of themselves using ethnic-religious maps which did not coincide with the national destinies they were declaring for those countries. What did Greeks stay on to do in Istanbul with the Turkish Republic? Was it, perhaps, to remember the defunct Byzantine Empire? And why were there still Turks in Salonika which became the second city in Greece?

In its own way and on a foundation of inequality, the Ottoman Empire really was a cohabitation of different nations. This happened under the control of a bureaucracy that was sometimes despotic towards all ethnic and religious groups in the violent atmosphere pervading many of its regions, especially in the framework of a confessional Islamic state. The Sultan was also the Caliph of Islam, the inheritor of an ancient institution which had an authoritative function in the *ummah*. The disappearance of the Caliphate in 1924 coincided with the end of the Osmanli dynasty, although the father of the new Turkey, Kemal Ataturk, at first seemed ready to leave it to at least the exercise of its religious responsibility. For more than eighty years, despite the aspirations of one kingdom or another, despite debates and congresses, Sunni Islam has not found an authoritative and unifying figure such as the Caliph, who remains without a successor. This is a problem whose significance the West has not grasped, but it is of great importance. As the British government could discern with its Islamic Indian subjects, the Muslims of the world experienced a great sense of frustration because of the ending of the Caliphate. A void had opened up in the exercise of authority in a community already deprived of a hierarchy. Today the abolition of the Caliphate comes round like a painful anniversary in the pronouncements of Osama bin Laden; perhaps, in his own way, he would like to fill the gap left by it.

In the Ottoman world, Muslims and non-Muslims, known as *dhimmi*, which indicated their subordinate and protected status, were not equals. In the framework of the authoritarian Muslim state, non-Muslim communities of *millet* status[1] lived as a sort of sub-state. The Orthodox (Greek, Arab, Slav, Romanian...) the Jews, the Armenians (and successively other communities) had their *millet*, in which the "patriarch" exercised religious and civil authority. In this we can see a structure for enabling multi-religious cohabitation. This is well worth remembering in a Europe where the Jewish minority was oppressed and the Muslim one was destroyed (remember fifteenth-century Spain). Yet Christian communities have survived in several regions conquered by Islam, although their numbers are diminished and, in North Africa, they have disappeared. These are the Oriental Christians, still to be found in Islamic countries today.

The difficult lives of non-Muslim communities, either through discrimination or oppression (also suffered by some Muslims), cannot conceal this picture of actual living together, even with all its inequalities. There were no Christian communities in the Maghreb, but there were quite a few Jewish communities. In the nineteenth century, the problems of the Jews, such as the accusation of that they performed

---

[1] The non-Muslim community was divided into *millets*, administrative units organized on the basis of religious affiliation rather than ethnic origin. The four *millets* were Armenian, Catholic, Jewish, and Orthodox, the latter being the largest and most influential. The *millets* enjoyed a fair amount of autonomy. At the head of each of these was a religious leader responsible for the welfare of the *millet* and for its obedience to the sultan.

ritual murders, came more from the Christians than the Muslims in the Ottoman Empire. Today, Jewish communities have disappeared from the Arab world, with a few very limited survivals, ghosts from the past to be seen in Old Cairo, Tunisia and Morocco. There were quite a number of losses due to a profound osmosis between Jews and Arabs, so much so that the Islamist Bernard Lewis spoke of a Jewish-Muslim civilization. About one million Jews left the Arab world after the Second World War. This happened as a result of a renewed upsurge of anti-Semitism, beginning before the birth of the nation of Israel and then subsequent to it. Thus a significant living together lasting over a millennium sank out of sight, as if swallowed up in some historic earthquake. Judaism represented an important and dignified form of religious faith. Without it the Muslims became more homogeneous, but they also became more isolated.

Even if Christians have seen a big reduction in their numbers throughout the Arab-Turkish-Iranian world in the twenty first century, Arab Islam still knows religious pluralism, thanks to their remaining presence. But Christians are emigrating, aware they can no longer live together with the Muslims who are ever more identity-conscious, and that they cannot accept being second-class citizens. In Israel and the Palestinian Territories, Christians are a sharply reduced minority. In the large country of Egypt, so influential in the Arab world, there is an important surviving Coptic Christian community, the most dense in the Arab world, which was effectively restructured from the 1960s, under Popes Cyril VI and Shenouda III. But the Greeks, Christian Arabs, and Europeans who made Egypt cosmopolitan left the country starting from the 1950s, at the time of Nasser's nationalizations. Egyptian racism, which took a dislike to the cosmopolitanism of Alexandria (just as Ataturk disliked the same thing in Istanbul), embodied the hegemonic Arab nationalism that ran from the 1950s to the 1970s throughout the Middle East.

The pressure of nationalism threw the cosmopolitan, multi-national and multi-religious constructions into crisis. Liberty was seen as national independence. This is the story of the nineteenth and twentieth centuries. And this story continued after the Second World War in the southern Mediterranean and in the decolonised parts of the world, continuing even after 1989. This history began at a brisk pace and has lasted for a long time. The Greeks, who were under Turkish rule, aspired aggressively to national independence from 1821 onwards. The Greek Revival is a model for other revivals in Europe, but above all it was aiming for the emancipation of the "nations" who were subject to the Sultanate. It was a very popular cause in the whole of Western Europe, and patriotic Italians watched and took part in it.

The Turks fought back and suppressed the Greek revolt. They hanged the Patriarch of Constantinople (a Greek who was the head of the Orthodox *millet*, and who was also opposed to Hellenic independence). However, an independent Greece did come into being, and represented a basic *vulnus*, a blow for Europe with its restoration of legitimate sovereignty. The Turks were unable to rein in the dissolution of the empire. Nationalism was like a worm eating it away through successive amputations. The hour of Serbia, Montenegro, and Romania would arrive and they were recognized as independent by the Treaty of Berlin in 1878. Next came Bulgaria, autonomous from 1878 and independent in 1908, and lastly there was Albania in 1912. The empire was no longer a framework for cosmopolitan living together. Its *millets* were turning themselves into nations: the Armenians were aspiring to independence, the Greeks were multiplying Hellenistic schools across Anatolia. The Ottoman powers in Istanbul had two pathways before them, either to defend the totality of the empire or to choose Turkification. It hesitated to take this latter route, so foreign to the Osmanli traditions, until the Young Turks came into government. They quickly understood the need to save the remaining territories and claim the rights of the Turkish nation. That is the tragic story of the final years of the empire that was buried by the first world war.

Even in independent Greece, things were not straightforward. Turks and Muslims were driven out to hellenize regions that had been occupied for centuries. Today mosques are no longer to be seen on the Greek landscape; at one time they were scattered throughout the whole country. From an ecclesiastical point of view, Christian Greece broke with the "Great Church of Christ", the orthodox patriarchate of Constantinople, deeming it to be subject to the Turks. The newly born Bulgaria had to "recleanse" itself from Muslims. In 1908 they made up 10% of the population, being largely Turks and Pomachi (Bulgarian-speaking Muslims). In 1985, under the Communist regime, this minority was forced into a process of Bulgarianization and, in 1989, 300,000 Muslims were forced to emigrate to Turkey (although half of these came back in 1990).

The Ottoman tapestry of nations had been the fruit of centuries of ethnic and religious stratification. In 1910, a city like Salonika, then the second city of Greece, was still home to 65,000 Jews living beside 35,000 Greeks and 30,000 Turks. It was the largest Jewish city in the Mediterranean. After annexation to Greece in 1912, the Greeks grew strongly, while the Turks diminished until almost disappearing in little more than ten years. Salonika had been the native place of the father of modern Turkey, Kemal Ataturk. Yet even this city was cleansed of its intricate weaving together of peoples. The final blow to its cosmopolitanism was inflicted by the Nazis during the Second World War, through the deportation and extermination of the majority of the remaining 45,000 Jews.

The great drama of the autumn of the Ottoman Empire took place in Turkish Anatolia but there were also important minorities involved. There were Greeks between Istanbul and the Aegean region, Armenians in the capital city and in the hinterland. There were Syrians and Chaldeans living towards the present-day borders of Syria, and there were Jews everywhere. Until the second decade of the twentieth century, Anatolia was pluralistic both ethnically and in religion – very different from how it is today. Non-Muslims made up a little more than 19% of the population. According to the Young Turks, it was necessary to save Anatolia from the clutter of non-Muslim minorities, such as the Armenians who, in some areas, might have been able to proclaim the birth of a separate state. During the First World War, there was a tragic ethnic cleansing, the systematic slaughter and deportation of the Armenians towards the Syrian desert. Out of the Armenian population of the empire, 70% died. According to some estimates, that meant more than a million individuals. The operation finished up hitting out at other Christians, such as the Syriac and Chaldean peoples. National passions were not enough to mobilize the population of Anatolia against the Armenians; the Young Turks needed to transform the nationalist struggle into a jihad against the giaour, the Christian unfaithful. Therefore, it was Christians in general who were hit, at least in some regions.

The massacre of the Armenians is the high point of a system used in the nineteenth and twentieth centuries to purify territories from ethnic and religious complications. This, the first genocide of the twentieth century, the Metz Yeghern (the great evil, for the Armenians), still awaits recognition by the government in Ankara, even at the level of its being a true piece of history. That is the genocide which Hitler was citing to his puzzled colleagues about the final solution of the Jews, when he said "Who, today, is still talking about the massacre of the Armenians?"

The "Grand Idea" of a Greece on both banks of the Aegean, which the Greeks were pursuing, brought about their defeat by the Turks after the First World War and also the elimination of a large part of the Hellenic population of Anatolia. The policy of Ataturk was to "Turkify" Anatolia. In 1881, Greeks and Armenians had made up 21% of the population of Turkey. The burning of Smyrna in 1922 and the enforced flight of Greeks and Armenians from that city (that meant two-thirds of the population) was the epilogue to the "Grand Idea" adventure, together with the ending of a cosmopolitan city where Muslims were in the minority. The exchanges of population between Greece and Turkey, following the Treaty of Lausanne in 1923, made Anatolia homogeneous, and destroyed Hellenic settlements that had lasted for millennia; they are the ones the West had come to know through *The Iliad*. Ethnic cleansing corresponds to the law of national homogeneity which all states practise to smaller or greater degrees, especially recently. The new Turkey of Ataturk wanted to be Turkish and mainly secular, but also Sunni Muslim.

Istanbul used to mirror the multinational character of the empire: in 1886 it contained 873,000 inhabitants, of whom 44% were Muslim, 17.5% Greek, 17.1% Armenian, 5.1% Jewish, 15.3% foreigners, plus some other small minorities. The city had a cosmopolitan character, as was evident in the Galata-Pera quarter, where the inhabitants were almost all non-Muslims, many being Europeans or people from the Far East. With the defeat of the Ottoman Empire, the Greeks had hoped to detach the city from the Turkish world, but that project was finished off by the failure of the "Grand Idea". The city became "Turkified". In 1932, the 690,850 inhabitants were mostly Muslim, whilst there remained 243,000 non-Turks. From the 1930s to the 1950s, the life of the ancient Ottoman capital was secularized: the Caliphate, the tekke of Muslim confraternities, and the social centrality of Islam were abolished by Ataturk. Traditional costume was no longer seen in the streets. Half way through the 1950s, the remaining Greek minority suffered another terrible blow because of the Cyprus crisis. Today there are about 2,000 Greeks in what they call the old Polis.

If the homogenization under Ataturk succeeded in respect of non-Muslims, it found its most powerful obstacles of all with the Kurdish minority, who are to this day reasserting their identity through the PKK (the Workers Party of Kurdistan) in Ocalan and through terrorism and political action. The spectre of pluralism, exorcized by the emigration of the Greeks and the massacre of the Armenians, has re-emerged with the Kurds and, in part, through an Islam which is not homogeneous since it is confraternal and Alewi, different from the majority Sunni Islam. Today, whilst the entry of Turkey into the European Union is under debate, the government in Ankara and Turkish society have yet to take account of the genocide against the Armenians. Also the same old spectre of pluralism is rising up in another guise in the Balkans. To homogenize and nationalize is more complicated than it seems.

Ethnic cleansing is accompanied by cultural change. In Turkey, the Armenian churches of Ani, not far from the border with Armenia, are abandoned ruins, and those neglected by Lake Van are mere memories, obliterated by the "Turkification" policy. For many years, the Turkish government has also objected to the presence of the Greek Orthodox Patriarchate on the banks of the Golden Horn, a reminder of Byzantium and a point of reference for world-wide Orthodoxy. But this is not just a problem in Turkey. At Bitola in Macedonia, I have seen how they preferred to knock down the mosques and pull down the minarets after the end of the Ottoman Empire. The same sad old story was repeated during the Yugoslav wars.

Erasing of the memory of people of a different faith and of most of their places of worship was a sign of the seizing of their territory. To destroy places of worship or to transform them into places for one's own faith is an act which symbolizes the violence that goes with the processes of forced homogenisation.

Ethnic cleansing is an ancient solution and has been practised many times. The Balkans have been a privileged territory for this sort of experience. Macedonia, a republic of former Yugoslavia, is also the Italian name for fresh fruit salad. There are many Balkan peoples living in that country: a Turkish minority, a strong Albanian minority, Jews, Serbs, Greeks, Bulgarians and the Macedonian majority. But who are the Macedonians? The Serbs considered them part of their own nation. The Bulgarians did the same. For the Greeks they were bastard Hellenes. Instead, Macedonian nationalism has claimed its own identity for over a century. In Macedonia today there is a grave problem of living together between the Macedonians and the Albanians, who are tempted by dreams of union with their other co-nationals in Albania and Kosovo.

Outside the Balkans, in the Middle East, the Israeli-Palestinian problem has been running for almost sixty years, a monument to the impossibility of living together. Every generation has experienced new pains, acts of aggression and sufferings, which persuade people still further about the impossibility of peace. Arab lack of realism and Israeli inflexibility have caused precious opportunities to be lost. The situation is complicated even from an ethnic point of view, with 1,283,000 Arabs holding Israeli citizenship in Israel (18.5% of the population of the country) and, on the other hand, 200,000 Israelis in settlements in the Palestinian Territories. It is hard to untie this knot which is not so much an ancient inheritance as the fruit of events after 1948 and 1967. We need not dwell on a question which is before us every day; yet it is one of the great problems of this century, and is constantly harped on as a great injury throughout the whole Muslim world.

Today attention is focused on Iraq. Public opinion takes note of the religious and ethnic complications of a country which many did not know about before recent events took

31

place. Iraq is an artificial creation by Winston Churchill and the British after the First World War, putting together Shiites in the south with Sunnis in the centre and Kurds in the north, who once formed one part of the old Ottoman Empire. In the same period a Kurdish state was refused, because of the weak international profile of that nation, and thus was laid down the basis of conflict across Turkey and Iraq and in parts of Iran and Syria as well.

In 1922, London put the Hashemite Prince Feisal on the throne, so as to save itself troops of occupation and to hand over a difficult country to an Arab sovereign. They had noticed the difficulty of governing the Mesopotamian arrangement directly and, drawing on their experience in India, the British preferred indirect rule. Iraq was a large-scale application of this. Thus was born the artificial construction that is Iraq. For eighty years it has lived under the hegemony of the Sunni minority, but today it finds itself having to take account of the wishes of the Shiites and Kurds as participants in the life of the country.

There was no shortage of complicated arrangements in the Middle East constructed in 1918, following the ending of the Ottoman Empire. The Lebanon is an example of this, but not because it was a mistake to create a state in which Christians and Muslims were in equal numbers, rather because the country had a greater role to play than its actual demographic weight would suggest. However, France, which held the authority of the Mandate and wanted to avoid a Lebanon that was too small in size, annexed to it areas inhabited mainly by Muslims; they had no fear of the Shiites at that time, because they were marginal and lacked influence. In present-day Lebanon, the Shiite community is the most numerous (a little under 40% according to some estimates). Half a century ago they were a depressed minority; today they have roused themselves through Islamic liberation and through their social solidarity networks to become politically the most influential faction. Simply because of demographic pressures, the Christians are finding themselves in the minority in a country created to guarantee their cohabitation with the Muslims on the basis of being in a majority.

Some stories from Europe

The construction of nation-states seemed the most modern and safe solution in Europe but it was not always the easiest; compromises had to be made. Sometimes people were assimilated and a name changed. Some groups in the population were deemed irrelevant. The borders of the nation-state seemed to guarantee an identity and security for a community which had the same national characteristics. This is the story, for example of the Italian Risorgimento against the Hapsburg Empire which was considered "the people's prison". United Italy has aspired to locate its boundary on the Alps, because this guarantees the country's security, despite the fact that it means swallowing up a conspicuously German-speaking Tyrolean community. German and Italian unification pushed the Hapsburg monarchy towards the south-east, accentuating its multi-ethnic and multi-religious character. Jews, Muslims, Catholics of the Eastern rite, Orthodox and Protestants were living in an empire of Latin-Catholic tradition.

As far as liberal opinion was concerned, the empire of Franz-Josef was an anachronism whose conflagration they expected. Its fate was to run through the typical crises when empires collapse. With its defeat in 1918, its various nationalities took their national destinies into their own hands by the means of creating or reinforcing different nation-states: Hungary, Poland, Austria, Czechoslovakia, Romania, Yugoslavia. Czechoslovakia preserved a link between Czechs and Slovaks, destined for divorce after the end of Communism in 1992. The history of Poland is of a land whose borders have been repeatedly remodelled and moved about. Yet Poland, as it was reborn after the first world war, shaped itself as a state which was by no means homogeneous. According to the 1921 census, the Poles made up barely 69%, followed by Jews, Ukrainians, and then Byelorussians and Germans. A city like L'vov, (L'viv or Lwow: depending on whether it was being named in Russian, or in Ukrainian, or in Polish) was in a region populated by Ukrainians, but with Poles most numerous in urban areas, alongside strong Ukrainian and Jewish elements, as well as a small Armenian group.

After the Second World War, the new Poland became more homogeneous within its new borders. Two-sevenths of the population had disappeared because of the war. The Holocaust had wiped out almost all the Jews, making a wilderness of a centuries-long history. The event of the displacement of the German and the Polish populations is a painful episode for some millions of Europeans, but is now closed with great realism by the new framework of post-war European culture which is no longer inclined to go in for national and territorial claims. It is a culture which has broken – hopefully for ever – with the logic of nationalism. And why not – when the Nazi claims for territories taken from Germany at Versailles were the origin of the Second World War and made the Holocaust a possibility?

In the history of our continent, there is one of the most senseless episodes of national homogenization: namely, the extermination of the Jews. This truly is the maddest expression of the cult of German racism. The Holocaust in Germany and Europe destroyed the cohabitation there had always been between Jews with Europeans and Christians. It was cohabitation that was part of European society, the German Jews were deeply assimilated, their destruction can find no justification, not even in the ideological paraphernalia which (even though absurd) motivates ethnic cleansing; it was said that they were a diversity that threatened the nation. The Nazi vision of a new order was the "scientific" ending of the mixing together of peoples (or, more precisely, of races). There was a hierarchy in which Slavs had a serving function, the Poles were seen as slaves, and down to an even lower level, the antisocial Gypsies and Jews – enemies par excellence – were condemned to elimination like some infection in society.

To achieve this project it was necessary to kill. The rhythm of assassinations and massacres perpetrated by Nazism in Germany and in Europe was incredible. The "Genocidal Nazi state" (according to Rudolph Rummel) killed about 21 million human beings, of whom one million were under 18 years old. For its part, the war that Hitler provoked caused almost 30 million dead, of whom more than 5 million were German. During the war, in the occupied territories, one in six Polish or Soviet citizens were killed in cold blood. It must also be recalled that, following the defeat of Germany and the national homogenization of the countries of the Eastern Bloc (Czechoslovaks, Hungarians, Poles, Romanians and Yugoslavs), 15 million Germans were also expelled. A good 1,800,000 met their deaths in this operation after the fall of the Reich. There was a huge "ethnic cleansing" in the heart of Europe, particularly desired by the Soviets. ("It has gone too far," said Churchill to his colleagues at Potsdam).

Auschwitz, where over a million Jews were killed alongside other Europeans, remains a warning monument against this insane, nationalistic and racist frame of mind. Out of Auschwitz came the new European consciousness, setting aside the logic of nationalism and, above all, learning the bitter lesson of its perversions. I have, in this sense, always been convinced that, if the European Constitution is to exert some kind of appeal to the conscience and the feelings of

Europeans, it must make Auschwitz its starting point and, therefore, the repudiation of anti-Semitism. The rituals to celebrate the 60th anniversary of the liberation of the extermination camps were not enough. Much history flows by and we cannot claim to keep the whole of it in mind, but it is vital to stress that Auschwitz remains a major turning-point which has caused an epoch-making change to our continent – Europe, where the Jews and so many European people lived through inhuman sufferings, and were all crushed by the logic of racial domination.

The end of colonisation and its legacy

We have passed somewhat rapidly over the crisis of living together in the European and Mediterranean areas. It is now necessary to investigate the end of centuries of cohabitation in the Russian and Soviet Empire, which sprang from a particular colonial expansion, because it was founded on the enlargement of frontiers. To this day, Moscow still exhibits the characteristics of a cosmopolitan imperial capital city. Even if the ex-Soviet states chose independence at the ending of the USSR with Gorbachov in 1992, every state still bears the traces of an "imperial" and multi-ethnic mingling; the Ukraine, for instance, accommodates an important Russian minority and a section of whose population is Russianized. The war in Chechnya is an example of how the independent nations of the ex-Soviet states have not resolved the problem of a mixture of people like that of the Russian Federation, of which Chechnya is one part. In every way, the whole of ex-Soviet territory is characterized, in different ways, by a degree of living together among diverse populations. The Caucasus is a crucible of ethnic identities and different religions. Ex-Soviet Central Asia stands out as an intricate complex of ethnic groups, along with Kazakhstan, where a third of the population is Russian, descendants of the emigration which accompanied Moscow's imperial expansion. And there is also the factor of the Muslim ex-Soviet republics, where ethnic groups meet one another across frontiers which are often artificial.

In Estonia, the government in Tallinn has discriminated against a large Russian minority, whose presence was bringing into question the national character of that new Baltic country. A law in 1992 deprived 37% of the population – the Russian speakers – of the right to vote, since it deemed them to be an expression of the policy of Russification. But can these Russians really be considered as foreigners? Rights are uncertain, when considering minorities such as this. One can discuss the acquisition of citizenship by immigrants in Europe, but these are displaced populations, the result of history, which creates factual realities. The racial ideology of Arab nationalism, caused by the shock of defeat by Israel, has for decades denied the right of the Jewish state to exist without negotiating with it, because the Jewish presence was the result of recent immigration, detrimental to the right of Palestinians. But the history of nations follows its own special courses. It is not always linear and respectful towards rights. Realism forces people to accept other people and to find ways of living together. Nevertheless, the wound can be so deep that no other solutions exist but to have an endless struggle. And the struggle distributes and attributes wrongs and rights, producing new legalities or illegalities.

One significant case, even if nowadays forgotten, is the exodus from Algeria of a million *pieds noirs* (French nationals, but by origin Italian, Spanish and Maltese) at the time it became independent in 1962. Along with them went another 200,000 Jewish Algerians, acknowledged citizens of France but having been in that North African country for centuries. The *pieds noirs* had begun arriving in Algeria in 1830, after the

French conquest. Their way of life was described by Albert Camus. That great novelist was also in favour of Algerian freedom and felt deeply over the dramatic exodus of people who were compelled to go back to a mother country which had often been foreign to them for whole generations. The war in Algeria from 1958 to 1962 was too bitter for there to be any hope of the Europeans and Algerians living together. Too many deep wounds had been inflicted, too much violence had happened on both sides. So when de Gaulle acknowledged the Algerians' right to self-determination, the *pieds noirs* emigrated to France in the space of a few days, even though they had been born in Algeria. Some were recent immigrants, others had been there for generations. It was their land where they had worked; yet it was also the Algerians' land which they considered to have been taken away from them for more than a century. The same pieces of land often had multiple ownership.

The exodus seemed an appropriate price to pay, because the origin of that community had been through colonialism. In the age of decolonization, the settlers had no rights, after having had many during colonial times. Yet, leading French people had not given up hope for cohabitation of Europeans and Muslims, and between Jews, Christians and Muslims, in spite of the sewer of hatred that divided the community so profoundly. This was what Camus hoped for: an attempt to live together in a new political framework. This was also the point of view of a person very different from the French writer; this was Cardinal Leon Etienne Duval, the Archbishop of Algeria, who had condemned the torture that the French used on Algerian militants during the critical period of the war. For Duval, people had to work at living together in a future political framework which would no longer be French Algeria. But both were swept away by the force of the hatred between the European and Algerian communities. While his faithful abandoned Algeria and the churches emptied to be transformed into Mosques, Cardinal Duval decided to remain in the country until he died: he believed in the value of trying to live together with the Muslims.

The permanence of a European community in decolonized countries was a great challenge. It was a fact of life inherited from colonialism, but it also gave an opportunity to the economies of the new states. Besides, colonisation had scattered Europeans throughout all the colonies, and this form of emigration was also favoured by the Indians or the Chinese (there are at least 20 million spread throughout the world).

The case of Southern Rhodesia, where a white government proclaimed itself independent from London in 1965, was a forcible solution for which the European Algerians would have longed. But these were solutions against the trend of history and the majority of the population. The President of Zimbabwe (ex-Rhodesia), Robert Mugabe, told me that the President and Liberator of Mozambique, Samora Machel, had advised him not to commit the mistake made in his own country, which had favoured the exodus of the whites at the moment of independence. Mugabe followed this advice for many years, so giving his country notable prosperity. However, the situation of Zimbabwe today, still under Mugabe, is very problematic, either through his policies towards the colonials or because of the absence of democratic procedures.

Decolonization has provoked some big crises for immigrant minorities. One thinks of the Indians settled in Uganda, but thrown out by Idi Amin: during his "reign": 300,000 people were killed. On the other hand, serious crises have arisen between ethnic and religious groups within the borders of ex-colonial countries. This is the distressing story of Sudan, with 2 million dead between 1983 and 2002, caused by the Northern Arabic-speaking people overpowering the Southern peoples (Christians and Animists). The same occurred in Rwanda and Burundi, and many other states

The ex-colonial states inherited artificial frontiers. In fact the borders of the colonies were often drawn without taking any notice of ethnic realities, but were negotiated and drawn up according to European interests and criteria. A remarkable proportion of the nation-states in the contemporary world have their origin in colonization. This is not only the case with fragile African states, but also with the giants of today's world, such as India, Pakistan, Indonesia or Nigeria. The last named was created by putting together diverse peoples and different religious communities through the actions of an able but harsh British representative, Frederick Lugard, between 1914 and 1919. The country still survives, in spite of persistent tensions and crises.

From India to South Africa

The Raj, India, the pearl of British colonialism – it gave the title "Emperor of India" to the monarch – is the source for the most dramatic story of division after the second world war. India, from the Punjab to Tamil Nadu, was a British creation which brought about a heterogeneous unity. For Gandhi, the great Indian tradition was a unifying factor, over and above the different religious and ethnic communities. Gandhian nationalism aspired to an independent India within the boundaries of the empire. The ideal of his party, the Congress Party, was democratic and secular. However, the Mahatma's dream was shattered by the birth of Islamic nationalism, which had neither ethnic nor linguistic nor even a territorial foundation, but fed upon the fear of Hindu dominance. Muslims were spread through the greater part of the empire and accounted for about 24% of the population; in Delhi it was 33% and less than 8% in the south. There were predominantly Muslim regions, such as East Bengal (today Bangladesh), the Punjab, Sind and Baluchistan. Islamic nationalism was less strong in these regions. However, among the Muslim minorities, there developed a fear that democratization would make Hindus dominant and be the sign of their complete marginalisation.

The Islamic movement was reinforced in the 1920s by the protest against the ending of the Caliphate and the request made to the English to become the defenders of that institution. In this way, Muslim identity was affirmed, giving Islam a basis for unity. Mohammed Ali Jinnah, the founding father of Pakistan, came from a region where Muslims were in the minority. He believed in separate destinies for Muslims and Hindus. Even during the 1930s, he theorized about the existence of two nations, and used to speak of "two different civilizations". After the war, British officials could not see their way to holding Hindu and Islamic nationalisms together. Therefore a decision for partition was made. Karl Meyer, writing about crises in empires, notes that partition "has been used repeatedly as an essential means of finding a short-term solution to problems". To start with it seems a practical choice, since it distinguishes the communities and gives effect to the principle of self-determination. But the true story is more complicated. Gandhi, Meyer continues, clearly foresaw the misfortunes that would result from the pragmatic surgery of partition.

On 15 August 1947, two separate states were born, Pakistan and India. Permanent tensions remain and have spilled over into a number of conflicts. In a short time a huge movement of population began between each of the countries: about 17 million people. In this turbulent period there were 300,000 dead (some suggest a larger number, up to a million). Kashmir remains a divided and disputed region, and, even today, Islamic fundamentalist theorists – as well as Pakistan – call it an unredeemed Muslim land. The act of partition signalled the failure of Gandhi's project; a state called Pakistan was founded on an Islamic basis. Its populations did not speak the same language; West Pakistan and East

Pakistan (now Bangladesh) have neither the same culture nor territorial continuity; on the contrary, each is thousands of kilometres apart from the other. At the moment of independence in West Pakistan, Mohajir – immigrants from India – made up a fifth of the population, about 6 million on top of 34 million.

India, with its Hindu majority, remains a multi-religious country, with a strong Muslim community of about 140,000,000 people. Founded upon an ancient civilization, whose continuity has been unbroken over a thousand years of development, it is remarkable for a powerful plurality of religions, ethnicity, and languages (Hindi speakers are officially only 40%). But, since 1947, India has been a democratic state. The great achievement of Jawaharlal Nehru was to resist communitarianism, and also to affirm a single state, something which India had never experienced in its history, and then he ran it in a democratic way. Nehru never gave in to the idea of Hindutva – Indianization – which would have been the equivalent of the concept of an "Islamic nation", an idea advocated by Savarkar, a nationalist, an unbeliever, and a great fan of Mazzini. Hindutva finds its support in the Hindu religious party, the BJP (Bharatya Janata Party) which governed the country between 1998 and 1999 and in 2004, following the crisis in the Congress Party. The history of India has been re-read through Hindutva eyes and has interpreted the complex civilization of India in a national-religious way, which, however, contains many inter-woven trajectories of thought and religion. The India of today is a country that is plural from every point of view, and irreducible to a single ethnic or religious item, but it has a single national destiny. It is the largest democratic population in the world, with the experience of more than half a century behind it, and so it is important for people who are asking themselves questions about cohabitation amid the diversities of the contemporary world.

Pakistan has progressively homogenized itself, basing itself upon Islam. The birth of the state required a strong emotional investment in Islam, different from what happened with Hinduism in India. The hundreds of thousands who died during the partition are held to be *Shahid*, Islamic martyrs; the Muslim immigrants are called *mohajir*, like the companions of the prophet who followed him into exile in Medina to found the first Islamic state. Islam is the decisive point of reference in a difficult and turbulent country at the crossroads of great international tensions (think of events in Afghanistan). In 1971, there were less than 3% of non-Muslims in West Pakistan.

Yet the Islamic foundation did not preserve the unity between West and East Pakistan. The latter proclaimed its independence in 1971 under the name Bangladesh, and it was supported by Indian troops. This is a story made little of in Western opinion, but it was extremely bloody. The Pakistani President Agha Mohammad Yahya Khan and his colleagues planned the destruction of the Bengali and Hindu élite in East Pakistan, together with the weakening of the economy of what was part of their own state. A million and a half Bengalis met their deaths in the Pakistani offensive in Bangladesh, whilst ten million were forced to abandon it and go to India. The non-violent struggle by the Awami League (Bengali) was harshly repressed by the Pakistan army. Military defeat, with Indian help, brought independence to the eastern part of Pakistan, the most densely populated part of the unitary state. In a time of civil and religious conflict, it is significant that secular India (mainly Hindu) and Muslim Bangladesh have taken as their national anthems two poems by the same great Bengali man of letters, Rabindranath Tagore, a Nobel laureate, supporter of independence and of the unity of Hindu India. He died in 1941.

Pakistan was the first Muslim country to be equipped with nuclear weapons (its "green" atomic policy was hailed enthusiastically by the Muslim world in 1998). Its testing came a few weeks after India had disclosed its own nuclear capability. Today, Islamic Pakistan is a problematic country, divided internally, with a strong and organised Shiite minority (between 15 and 25%), but also fertile ground for Islamic extremism, especially in the development of its madrassas, Qur'anic schools financed by the state. The minorities, the Christians (about 1.5%) and the Ahmadiyya, a Sunni schism, are often scapegoated by those asserting a pure, tough Islam. Consider the law on blasphemy against Islam, which is used to strike at the Christians.

Pakistan also presents a great problem for security from terrorism. As Jean-Marie Colombani wrote, "it is a great cauldron and at the same time a kind of great factory for making fighters in the holy war. The most radical ideology radiates from here." This is why, following 11 September, the United States has intensified its level of attention to Musharraf's government, pressuring him to take action against radical Islam and terrorism. On the other hand, an unpublicized military collaboration also began in 2005 between India and the United States. A vast, completely nuclearized geopolitical game was started in the Indian subcontinent, although hampered by the old divorce, sixty years old and still causing pain.

The partition between India and Pakistan, with 17 million displaced from one country to the other, represents the biggest divorce of the twentieth century and also the largest "ethnic cleansing". The lesson that comes from this rapid and uneven review of events is that the nation-state is the crucial location for giving security to a population. Yet it is no simple matter to understand what is meant by "national", or at least the meaning is not the same everywhere: what did it mean for Pakistan in 1947? But nations are created, as happened in that most risky piece of contemporary national construction which gave birth to a new state in the ancient land of the Torah and draws the Jews of the world together from extremely diverse backgrounds.

The nation-state is sometimes the outcome of ethnic cleansing, assimilation, and the displacing of people. Following any other course often seems impossible. Nevertheless, some present-day states have chosen to do just that. This is the road on which Mandela's South Africa set out, when he was released in 1990 after twenty-six years in prison. The leader of the ANC (African National Congress) declared himself in favour of a country that was free and multi-racial. Although it had no shortage of difficulties, a process of negotiation brought about a peaceful transition from apartheid to a democratic and multi-ethnic regime. In 1994 Mandela was elected president. It was one of the greatest peaceful transitions of the second half of the twentieth century, on a par with the liberation of Poland from the USSR. The process allows for the white South African minority to remain with an African government, alongside other minorities and with a variety of African peoples.

In contrast, the apartheid policy had aimed at ethnicizing the various groups, confining them to Bantustans, a type of ethnic state covering 13% of the national territory. The trend towards "separate development" of the races by means of the Bantustans tended to reduce the demographic influence of black people, to break them up into different national identities, and to assure the whites control of the useful territory (1.87% of the land). Because of its economic development, this territory also attracted most of the Africans, who were, however, considered to be immigrant foreigners or second-class citizens. And yet, in this South Africa of many identities, there still existed a sense of common nationality. Apartheid, for its part, caused the non-whites to find themselves thrown together, despite the ethnic differences on which South African policy had been constructed. Learning from Gandhi and watching the struggles of Martin Luther King, Mandela was convinced – as he wrote in his autobiography – that "the whites were also Africans just like the others and that the majority would need the minority in any future government. Be assured, we have no intention of throwing you back into the sea." The majority needs the minority, or the minorities.

History offers us no lessons and no formulae. In the twentieth century, the creation of some nation-states has imposed ethnic cleansing. By contrast, in other cases – such as Iraq – no notice has been taken of the realities of a composite population, suppressing the differences. The problem of living together with others has been resolved by separation, by the construction of homogeneous states or by the marginalization of minorities. However, with the dawn of the twenty-first century, the problem is posed yet again. There are unsolved situations, or new situations created, maybe by displacing population or by emigration. Above all the problem now arises in a world where distances have been shortened, cultures have been brought closer together and frontiers have experienced substantial opening up.

Chapter 2

GLOBALIZATION
AND IDENTITY

Two empires and the Third World

It is not easy to understand the contemporary world. It is complex and confusing. People often speak about "a new world disorder". We were used to thinking about the world along the lines of the cold war: one part being "good" and the other "bad". Through those lenses, we could explain so many things: even the war between North and South Vietnam. Everyone's position depended on a choice between the two worlds. East and West corresponded with the culturally rooted idea of Orient and Occident. The world was moulded into two empires and "two civilizations"; this phrase was a recurring theme in electoral campaigns. Who does not remember the "evil empire" of Ronald Reagan? There were disturbances in some regions of the empires: consider the Hungarian crisis of 1956, the Czechoslovak in 1968 or the Soviet invasions of Afghanistan, also the revolutionary movements in Central America or the question of Cuba. Wars by proxy broke out between the two powers. But, despite all its complexities, the system was underpinned by a clear, explained set of directions. The world seemed divided into two.

Many identities, nationalities, ethnic and religious groups were compressed into the two empires and they counted for little within the logic of each bloc. This appeared to be the case especially in the Communist part of the world. Many national questions were forgotten in Eastern Europe: and there were dominating questions that would emerge after 1989. In quite a few countries, mostly of Eastern Europe but also in the countries of the West (Italy among them) there was talk of more or less "limited sovereignty" in regard to the policies of the two empires. If one knew where to look, national issues even existed in the Soviet world, but they were hidden away.

However, the frontiers of the two blocs did not cover the whole of the globe. Between the two empires there was a third world, made up of the non-aligned countries. In 1955, ten years after the end of the Second World War, when the cold war was at its height, the first conference of 29 Afro-Asian countries, including India and China, was held in Bandung, a city in Indonesia. The conference affirmed self-determination for nations, struggle against colonialism and non-alignment to the blocs. The non-aligned movement did not have a rigid identity, because it deemed countries to be West-friendly or Soviet-friendly. However, it initiated a third position between the two blocs, where ex-colonial states could locate themselves, and keep their distance from cold war thinking. For many countries, this was a background against which they could display their own identity, which was taking its first uncertain post-decolonization steps on the world scene and within its own national boundaries. For the most part, this was defined as the "Third World", an expression put forward in 1952 by the demographer Alfred Sauvy and modelled on the *Tiers État* of the French Revolution. By translating it into English as "Third World", he softened the historical and revolutionary allusion to mean the part of the world which was neither socialist nor western.

Was this a new position in the global politics of the cold war? Some people think that it could have exercised a revolutionary function. Frantz Fanon, a revolutionary from the Antilles, but on loan to Algeria in the struggle for liberation, had theorized about a revolution against imperialism by the new world proletariat, the citizens of the south, and "the wretched of the earth". The countries of the east, China and those on the Left in the western world supported movements for liberation from colonialism. The more revolutionary areas of the Third World theorized and practised a strategic alliance with Communist countries. The Third World was a "world" under construction, in no way an organic whole. For some people, well endowed with illusions, they represented the future.

The Catholic and socialist Julius Nyerere, founder and President of Tanzania, searched for a new economic way between Marxism and capitalism. Another person, like the mad dictator Sekou Toure in Guinea, aimed for socialism amid international isolation. For Mobutu's Zaire, western-friendly and corrupt, the road was to be African authenticity. We could go on with more examples. The father of Senegalese independence (one of the few African leaders to lay down power of his own free will), Leopold Sedar Senghor, had theorized about *la negritude*, the original African character, to be placed alongside but not opposed to European identity. There were great efforts put into recovering African traditions, (which were not always written down or to be found on monuments), aiming to find and legitimize identities for several of the countries in that continent.

In the post-war years, and above all in the 1960s, many people were faced with becoming subjects of new nations on the world scene. They had to say who they were both to themselves, to their neighbours and to the whole world. Non-alignment and Third-worldism were a background against which to work out new identities. In the years of decolonization, millions of men and women began to call themselves citizens of a nation, adhering to a collective identity and defining themselves as opposed to others. They believed in the historic role of their countries. From the 1950s, the masses of the southern part of the world began to live through

49

a time of passionate participation in political life. They were called upon to participate, mostly in a non-democratic way. This is the history of the feelings of millions of human beings who, in a few decades, entered into a landscape of political passions, the like of which their parents had never known. They looked with hope to the future, believing it possible to become free from poverty and marginalization. They felt they had a destiny to struggle for in their history. This history is largely yet to be written; it is intense and absorbing.

Today, this "third" world, which so fascinated some sections of western thought, is over. Often it failed politically and economically, a failure which was acknowledged after 1989. With the ending of the Soviet empire, non-alignment has lost its raison d'être. The conflict of interest between East and West had increased the strategic value of many countries, such as those in Africa, who had been courted by the two empires. After 1989 all this was to go into a dreadful decline. Strategic interests had bolstered non-viable regimes, such as the Somalia of Siad Barre or the Ethiopia of Menghistu. After 1989, every country had to validate itself. The Asiatic countries did this by taking their decisions on economic grounds.

The end of the Third World after 1989 was accompanied by the failure of many countries from the economic viewpoint. This compelled them into the politics of tough economic reorganization based on market criteria. Non-alignment had been an openly Afro-Asian and ex-colonial movement. From the 1990s, the affairs of Africa were very different from those of Asia, which had behind it age-old, rich civilizations with their settled forms of expression. The main difference may have been economic, but it was not the only one. The idea of non-alignment, launched at Bandung in 1955, was that ex-colonial Asiatic and African countries should together seek for a common future. This idea had now been set aside. Besides, when well understood, even colonization had been shaped differently in sub-Saharan Africa, in Asia and in the Arab world. In the 1960s, the great Italian Orientalist, Giuseppe Tucci, had already written, "The major event that we are witnessing today is the entry of Asia into history: I would say that, until yesterday, Asia endured history but today is in the front rank of making it." This evaluation does not relate to Africa.

The Third World finished with the ending of the Communist empire. Not only did a position in international affairs disappear, but a world-view which included many national identities simply disappeared, often starting with their artificial boundaries and their weak state structures. Marxism had had a role in the definition of these identities. Sometimes it served as a language for the management of power by the new ruling classes, in the absence of any other political culture or when faced with a refusal to embrace Western liberal democracy. The role of local traditions was conspicuous and sometimes rewritten in the light of the new political situation. The end of the cold war was a rude awakening for the Third World countries. Many of the Asian ones found their way ahead, but those in Africa are going through a period of uncertainty. The African states – opened up to democracy and market forces – are experiencing an identity crisis as they undergo the reorganization of their structures. Sometimes they discuss national identity, as happens in the Ivory Coast, a country which has had a stable economic and political situation, or as happens in the huge Congo where the very unity of the nation is at risk. Since the 1990s Africa has been living amid profound turbulence.

Identity and globalization

Globalization and the end of the cold war have put all identities under discussion, not just those in the ex-Third World. As new horizons open up and old scenarios are overthrown – however protective and limiting they may have been – identities are once again up for discussion and are being redesigned. This is the process which characterised the 1990s, and we are still deep in it. I do not intend to discuss globalization – there is already such a vast literature about that – I am simply recalling how the process of globalization has called so many identities into question. In his seminal essay on art in the era of the conquest of America, Serge Gruzinski has thrown light on how Europe in the sixteenth century and Mexico have experienced a great period of globalisation through the conquest. The redefining of identities was very powerful, particularly through an intense cultural cross-fertilisation which produced many works of art in Europe and Mexico. This cultural cross-fertilisation was the fruit of the "globalization" of the conquest and is the enthralling theme of Gruzinski's book, whose precise title is *La pensée metisse*. It is the cultural history of the conquest, which produced cross-fertilization in America and powerful repercussions in Europe.

Colonization, especially in the nineteenth and twentieth centuries, was a process of globalisation which created new horizons for entire regions of the world. Jean-Loup Amselle, a French anthropologist alert to African society, observes how Africa had lived through several globalisations. Colonization was the most radical, but there have also been Christian and Islamic missions which have profoundly altered the world-view for several human groups. They were thrust into new horizons, those of the imperial colonials, of Christianity and the *ummah* of Islam. Radical rethinking had been imposed on them. Ethnic, religious and cultural identities were reconstructed and adapted and they underwent a deep process of osmosis. They reordered their own existence on new horizons different from the one they had had before and distinguished by their expansion of view.

Ethnic identity in Africa is often thought to have a character that comes from far away, from the mists of the time before colonization. But it was in part created by colonial administrators and ethnologists, who classified, defined and isolated in order to govern. There were classifications of peoples who had lived until then in other world-views. They saw themselves assigned an ethnic identity according to the categories made by the colonial administrators or by European ethnologists. Insisting on different characteristics of one group from another was useful for governmental purposes, for giving a good understanding of their subjects and also for what caused divisions among them. The meeting between the imported classifications of colonial culture and local realities sometimes caused rigidity of identities. Colonial globalisation obliged fluid identities to define themselves. The religious universalisation of Christianity and Islam nudged people into feeling they were part of a community of believers which was much vaster than their local faiths. They had been condensed into the one category of Animism, as if that were a third religion alongside Islam and Christianity.

Present day globalization is very different from its predecessors, if for no other reason than it is more universal and more rapid. It is also imposing restructuring processes on intricate identities and profound historical roots. As I have already noted, with the ending of Communism, there has been an upsurge of dominant nationalist identities which had mostly been lying dormant. Some years ago I was struck by the criticism levelled by some Polish professors against the integration of their country into the European Union. They said that it was "A necessity but, nevertheless, Poland had only regained her own liberty a short time before and so it was now difficult to become part of a new grouping." In Albania, once Communism was finished, following the terrorist dictatorship by the national-communism of Enver Hoxha (perhaps the most terrible regime of all in Eastern Europe), conflicts flared up between groups whose identity had seemed to have been lost in the past – for example, between North and South – and a language problem also arose.

The history of former Yugoslavia is a bloody affair concerning the resurrection of identities and the birth of new nations. Nobody could ever have thought that a Bosnian-Muslim identity existed. And besides that, as I have already remarked, the identifying category of Muslims in the Indian Empire was invented so that Pakistan might be founded and their destiny could be separated from that of India. In general terms this reconstruction of identities has firstly been those of religion for the purpose of legitimizing nations, but it has also been a trans-national phenomenon. After 1989 and to the great surprise of the secularization theorists, who had been foreseeing their extinction more or less slowly, religious identities and the communities which they inspire are now playing a leading public role.

These identities have not always been constructed in a calm way. They cause conflicts with neighbours, or at least with those who oppose them. Benjamin Barber was not far from the truth in his *Jihad versus McWorld*, singling out the resumption of fundamentalist and integrationist movements as a reaction to globalization. "McWorld" means a method of production, a globalized system of living, a mixing together of cultural forms which have their heart and genetic base in the United States. In fact, globalization often implies Americanisation or Westernization and this provokes strong reactions. Identity is defined by contrast with others, with foreigners. Barber concludes, "It promotes community but at the expense of tolerance and interaction and it creates a world in which belonging is still more important than the power of its citizens."

This reaction identified by McWorld is not only Islamic fundamentalism, typified by the image of the young radical

Muslim wearing Nike shoes. This reaction cuts across many identities, national, ethnic, religious and cultural. A similar awareness from a religious standpoint was to be found in the Orthodox Patriarch of Constantinople, Athenagoras, born 1886, died 1972. He was a Greek from the Balkans who witnessed the undoing of the Ottoman Empire and the crisis of the nations. After the war he found himself squeezed by the Greek-Turkish conflict and besieged by the Cyprus crisis. It is sometimes possible to perceive very clearly the deeper currents of history from observing religious communities. In the 1970s, Athenagoras noted a contemporary tendency: "On the one hand, we have the advent of planetary man in a history that is becoming worldwide, and on the other, maybe to escape the impersonal quality of industrial society, every nation is clinging to its own distinctive origins."

Muslims faced with Westernization have felt they must express afresh who they are by recovering their Islamic roots. The great religious communities have to re-present their identities, faced with secularization and life-styles which are a great departure from traditional values. African states, no longer supported by Third World interconnections, are compelled to reaffirm their identities in a way based on the ethnic and religious identities of their citizens, disaffected from national patriotism. Not wishing to die crushed between a globalized world and the majority of the state, they feel the need of a new self-definition and hopefully to have trans-national links. A large country such as China, anxious about its unity, is feeling the need to make a new approach to its ethnic and religious minorities. We can see this, for example, in the founding of the Research Institute for ethnic minorities, promised by Jiang Zemin after the events of 9/11 and charged by the Council of State (the Chinese government) with the task of investigating this complex reality inside modern China.

In considering this process of practical reorganization, it is necessary to take account of the great void left by the crisis in Marxism. There is a lack of studies into the "secularization" of the greatest of "secular" religions, Marxism. This was an ideology that made connections embracing Communist countries, western Communist parties, liberation movements, critical western intellectuals and many others as well. It offered a "global" vision of the world and of the future and also served as a grammatical form by means of which the ruling class could be organized and the political situation could be discussed. Even if the Marxist perspective is finished with, it should nevertheless be understood how the methods of the Marxist movements have been strongly assimilated into other political cultures: Marxism after Marxism needs to be understood. We find traces of it in ideologies, in the way that politics is carried out, in the theology of Islamic liberation of Ali Shariati, who co-ordinated Iranian Shiitism and its study in Paris during the 1970s, and, with notable success, affirmed the revolution of Imam Khomeini. It may be that the Christian theology of liberation has played a minor historic role compared with that of Islam.

The drift to fundamentalism does exist. But it is not the only response to globalization. However, Islamic fundamentalism was not born in the 1990s; it has roots in an ancient crisis for Islam when confronted by Europe and later, since the 1920s, it has found a first social and political realization in the Muslim Brotherhood. Therefore fundamentalism is not solely religious, but is sometimes ethnic, even if it deals with more restricted phenomena. Remember Basque terrorism, with its fundamentalist cult of race and territory and also its cult of death.

Globalization is not merely a necessity imposed by the present times, but a great opportunity for reformulating one's own identity inside the framework of a wider horizon and to state who we are vis-à-vis our neighbours and the world. As I have said, this is an opportunity which involves not just hard opposition but also the expounding of a topic which is now being re-elucidated. It is a political and cultural opportunity in our own time, and should not be seen as simply a threat, but also as a possibility. This demand is being made by political culture and by commentators. In Europe, national identities are mainly rooted in the unification process among the European nations. The states of Europe are saying who they are in the wide world of globalization. At the same time they are realizing that they are no longer adequate in the face of the challenges of the immense dimensions of the world, of vast markets, of peace, of struggle against terrorism, and in facing up to Asia. National identities are being re-cast, but with reference to the Union.

Every European can see the flag of the Union next to their own flag. In countries like Italy this is seen today more often than it was fifteen years ago. Through symbolism, the identities of European states are being shown to relate to a larger grouping. This also reveals an awareness of being Europeans, which is spreading among the French, Germans, Belgians, Italians and Spanish. In regions of the world where the European presence is thin, it is taken for granted that the citizens of the Union do feel they belong to something which they possess in common. It remains to be seen how the real political development of the Union will actually go over the coming years.

Nothing will save us from the risks of conflict, opposition, and an urge to separate ourselves in order to assert ourselves. Even in the framework of tried and tested European culture, immunised by two world wars in the twentieth century, there are still negative nationalist reactions against the process of unification, together with a resurgence of local passions. Ours is a long and delicate transition, conditioned by the economic processes of a globalized world, and also by those cultural and identity factors which a Marxist cast of mind had already defined as secondary superstructures twenty years ago.

The world of McWorld comes from a point of view which is more homogenous and more 'one and the same' than that of the past, yet – and this is a paradox of our times – it also promotes the development of profound differences. The world is more the same and more differentiated at the same time. Certainly, when I discuss identities, I line up examples that are not homogenous with one another, not even in size, such as Islamic fundamentalism, renascent patriotism in Croatia, crises of identity in some African countries, the new American arrogance, the rediscovery of their religious identity by Catholics in our own time, and Russian nationalist sentiment… yet, there is a general cultural climate which is leading to the re-casting of identities and to new enthusiasm to take part in them.

Identities, not destinies

There is no need to have an over-deterministic view of identity. There is a fatalism about identity which does not correspond to reality. That fatalism can be found in some features of the works of Samuel Huntington, although he is praiseworthy in other ways. Islam is not predestined to be in confrontation with the West because of its deep religious identity. Identities or, if you will, civilizations are not natural destinies, they are expressions of the choices of human beings and their cultures, the political wishes of groups of leaders, the living conditions in a particular area of land, and by the power of relationships… Identities are not the nature of a self-consistent group that works like a mechanism. There are no destinies that cannot be questioned as some often claim or suggest.

Culture, debate about ideas and common consensus all have strength in this globalized world. This is an element of hope: the ability to discuss, think and advocate. The "steamroller" of globalization does not flatten everything, nor does it wield an irresistible power of coercion. There is resistance that comes from culture; there are creative forces which arise from identities that have been revived and reinvented. Eric Hobsbawm, a Marxist-leaning British historian, has demonstrated how distinctive traditions may be constructed, even, he would say, invented. Inventing a tradition does not mean a piece of falsification, although this might be said naively. It is something more than that. As Agostino Giovagnoli has written in a beautiful essay dedicated to *Storia e globalizzazione*, "In globalization, pressures to validate the local dimension or ethnic identity develop in the void left by crises in traditions which seek to become revitalised in folklore mode, or even by ad hoc invention."

We do find ourselves faced with a crisis in transmitting traditions and memories, and also about reintroducing them in an unedited and often very spontaneous form. Elegantly, Hobsbawm suggests that the greater part of collective identities is like T-shirts which people put on like a skin they have rediscovered.

This phenomenon of community consciousness in daily living does not show itself in a clear-cut way. Jean-Loup Amselle asks, "Can we truly know what is our own skin and what is clothing?" The process of re-Islamization among the Arab élite who had shared so passionately in the national socialism of Nasser or in lay Pan-Arabism took place by means of individual and group choices, which donned new mental and material clothes, even if they were, in a manner of speaking, interwoven with an ancient tradition and religious faith on secular roots, going beyond time itself. There is undoubtedly a rediscovery and reorganizing of tradition, when people's own identity is being reaffirmed.

Especially since 1968, European culture has lived through a profound break-down of the very idea of tradition. That year saw the last great turmoil in Western Europe, a political revolution which very soon failed and was reabsorbed. Nevertheless, this did signal an anthropological revolution which profoundly changed the habits of many Europeans, bringing a revision of relationship with the past and also its own anti-institutional agenda. Tradition was contrasted with emancipation, a classic opinion which the movement of 1968 spread among the general population. Today, while Europe rethinks its identity once again, it is measuring itself against its traditions. Every rediscovery of tradition is a reinterpretation of it. Identity founded on tradition is the fruit of one's relations with the present moment.

In the 1960s, the Roman Catholic Church felt the need to redefine itself in its theological and spiritual awareness vis-à-vis the contemporary world. This is why it had convened the Second Vatican Council, which produced several documents dedicated to other (non-Catholic) people, another addressed to the modern world, another to non-Catholic Christians and another to non-Christian religions, without forgetting some reflections on atheism. Never, in the long history of Councils, had "others" received so much space in a re-thinking of Catholicism. Was this a secularization of Catholicism? It does not seem so, because, although it was travelling through a series of crises, the Church reaffirmed its own profound identity, as we can see from the two most recent Popes, John Paul II and Benedict XVI. This is a re-expounding of identity through both tradition and awareness of the contemporary world.

Some years ago, a Franco-Lebanese novelist, Amin Maalouf, who was sensitive to the crossover points between culture and religions in the Mediterranean, made an attentive investigation into identity. He observed that each person is the receiver of two inheritances: one is vertical and comes from history and tradition, the other is horizontal and comes from the present day. The latter has a powerful effect. The stimuli from globalization work precisely in the dimension of this contemporaneity. Even if we often think that the traditional roots of identity are prevailing, there is an undoubted attraction from the contemporary world which must not be undervalued. Identities are often held to be like an inheritance, but they themselves undergo deep saturation and radical alterations through the filter of the contemporary scene. Contemporaneity either pressures us into homogeneity or, contrariwise, can favour differentiation.

Maalouf explains the current outbreak of the contrasting styles in this way, "The truth of the matter is that if we put a great deal of rage into asserting our differences, this is actually because we are becoming ever less different… Despite our conflicts and our age-old enmities, every day that passes reduces our differences a little more and makes our affinities grow a little more." We are indeed more similar than we were. To see this all we need to do is take a look at the young people of the most recent European generation. National differences which were strong two generations ago, are now considered secondary. So much growing closer to one another leads either to assimilation or to living together without conflict; and yet it also has the paradoxical effect of promoting differences and conflicts.

At the present time traditions are being rethought and recovered. As we have already emphasized, such a process plays a powerful part in the working out of culture. We must also underline the new role taken on by religions in giving or confirming identities. On the other hand, contemporaneity creates tidal waves of ideas, passions and fashions which reach many people in the world, at least those who are connected to systems of communication. On occasion, these waves are so powerful that they create a disoriented kind of human being who has been deprived of a traditional identity. Tzvetan Todorov (who knew both the Communist East and Western Europe) has written of how contemporary men and women of that sort react because of this lack and they gain themselves an identity through choices or by making attachments that turn them into participants in a collective "We", and this becomes a starting-point in their approach to the world at large.

But contemporaneity also means an awareness that we share in a situation with people in other groups and yet they are still considered to be foreigners and separated. In Europe, the experience of Chernobyl, a Soviet atomic power station which exploded on the 26th April 1986, has revealed how the damage did not stay within the frontiers that divided the Communist from the Western world. Equivalent reflections could be drawn about climatic or environmental difficulties which involve everybody. Even terrorism, which is blind as to whom it attacks, strikes people of very diverse extractions. In Madrid in the attack on 11 March 2004, the dead in the station at Atocha "represented" the whole world, not just Spaniards whom the terrorists regarded as guilty for military intervention in Iraq. There were Muslims from various countries, Latin Americans and people from the East. Modern cities, and not only those in Europe, are home to people of all kinds of origin and religion. They are truly multicoloured.

Contemporaneity means living together in the same places, but, above all, it means common involvement in the tides of the times and in the same events. We can perceive a common time which exists over and above the destinies of diverse peoples and geographical distance. We are clearly dealing mostly with indirect signs and events of the times, and therefore with a selection of them. However, the people of the world are networked together and feel themselves included in some events, all living simultaneously, with the same feelings and common reactions. The tragic events of 11

September 2001 in New York were felt simultaneously via television. Jean-Marie Colombani, editor of *Le Monde*, translated our collective involvement in the drama in New York with the phrase "we are all Americans". World public opinion became immensely involved in the tragedy of the tsunami in Asia at the end of 2004, although it was an event far away from Europe or America; but there were many non-Asian tourists in the area at the time. The aid collection was at an individual, not only governmental level. It showed the involvement of people in a drama that they followed hour by hour on television and wished to do something about, however remote from them it might be. Great world events reveal an awareness that we are contemporaries through the synchronization of our feelings and attention. Yet we must remember that contemporaneity does not produce the global, cosmopolitan man or woman.

These observations about tradition and contemporaneity – and one could add many more – do not solve the problem in which we are placed. Indeed they complicate it, because they show how intricate are the ways of constructing one's own identity. The great world-scale liberalizations have not brought about the triumph of individualism, but rather reinforced and developed the identities of various groups. These identities are the children of their history and tradition or its recalling, yet they must also take account of being contemporaries in a "culture" of globalization, as regards stimuli, passions and events that transcend the borders of groups or countries.

Diverse but not pure and isolated

We are in a season of the rebirth of identities. But we are also in a time of strength in global ebbs and flows and in contemporaneity. It will therefore prove hazardous and dangerous if we isolate one identity from the other. When such isolation comes about, we find ourselves facing a process which is unnatural, aggressive and dangerous. Thinking oneself to be alone, separate and hostile constitutes that *pureté dangereuse* spoken of by Bernard-Henri Levy. This "dangerous purity" has been the origin of very many processes of separation and conflict. It is the key claim of every fundamentalism over and against a "dirty" and polluting world, over and against what is being set out as the pure and the desirable. It is an ethnic, ideological and racial claim which publishes its own purity and points out the polluting threat in others. It announces its own "pure" identity by marginalizing or destroying others with the same violence that is shown against itself.

No identity – even national ones – coincides with frontiers, but is located in a great texture and finds itself amid a variety of components. We are diverse, but we are not so separate as we might want to believe we can be through efforts at cultural or physical isolation. There is no community which can call itself homogeneous and "pure" without distorting itself and its history or by sealing itself off completely. Homogeneity and purity are frequently an invention such as that which has preceded the birth or the recognition of some nations. Thus, racial purity is an invention, like the invention of the Italian race by Fascist "scientists" in 1938. The dangerous activity of separation develops in societies or environments where common characteristics are blurred and traits have become mixed, while differences are being honoured. In an authoritative work which is severe concerning identities, the Italian anthropologist Francesco Remotti has observed, "The arts of separation in the technological field, in the processes of purification, in the personnel field, in the techniques of analysis, in the intellectual field, all indicate modes of behaviour which, sociologically speaking, give rise to a fairly restricted perspective within which the 'germ of purity' (whatever that means) may nestle and flourish."

It is more than a decade ago since we saw the rise and prospering of the "germ of purity" in certain situations. Purity is the totalitarianism of human identity; and I am not here indulging in some myth of a single global and cosmopolitan society. Identities exist, arise and are necessary for living and they are the children of history. As Benedict XV, the Pope in the First World War, used to say, "nations do not die". And likewise other identities do not die, even if they can change. But, on the other hand, no one lives any more – or rather they live less and less – in a single nation with a single group identity. All the time, every identity becomes less absolute. This is true of individuals in the existential sense; but also at the national, state or community level. Once and for all, we cannot isolate ourselves.

Perhaps each one of us carries more than one identity within us, even if we do it at different levels. American Catholics were rebuked for being less loyal to their country because they depended on the Pope, a foreign monarch. Jews used to be rebuked as unfaithful citizens of their native country, firstly for their faith and later for their Zionism. Those are two classic instances of thinking that is unable to accept the profundity of real life. One could continue with a series of examples to illustrate how each one of us may have various identities to which we refer: so inside ourselves, there is already a living together. Todorov wrote, "Today – one way or another – each of us has lived out, in ourselves, a meeting of cultures: we are all cross-breeds… Belonging to a national culture is only the strongest influence of all, because of the marks, derived from family and community, language and religion, all mixed together in our body and mind." It is as if we have a cross-breeding of identities inside of us.

Sometimes, just to react to this personal complexity, an individual needs to shout out loud one exclusive identity. This is the cry of the "disoriented man" in the contemporary world, but it does not do justice to the complexity that he is carrying in himself and taking into his relationships with other people.

Neither can we be isolated from the point of view of national identities and groups. Not only is every identity not pure, but it develops within a tapestry of changes and relationships with other people. Europeans, who for centuries have fought dramatically among themselves, have now discovered that they are similar, share general interests and indeed, have so much in common. Community of interests is not just a new fact, it comes from long ago. Identities do not die; however, making them exist does not mean isolating them or purifying them. We all live in a woven tapestry, in a civilization, in a system of changes and meeting points. This tapestry makes us all cross-breeds or at least necessarily adjacent to one another, because it throws into relief whatever is held in common, and yet it does not annul diversity of characteristics.

As has been said many times, this is the common experience of the Europeans in the 21st century. But a sense of community also exists among the "black" Africans. The construction of the African Union is founded on a sense of community. And there is a sense of community among Latin Americans, despite the ironies about differences between one group and another – something that happens within nations. Since its origin, Christianity has tended to affirm – as Paul of Tarsus taught – that there is no Jew, no Greek, no barbarian, but all are one in the Christian faith. Paul does not emphasize cultural similarities but he insists on the community of faith which brings all identities together into the destiny of "the people of God". One could speak of the cultural affinity of the Anglo-Saxon world which exists between Australia, Canada, Great

Britain and the United States. These are all communities at different levels, and, at the same time, they deny "purity" and the isolating out of any one identity.

The differences remain. They do re-emerge, sometimes in a virulent form. But this neither obscures nor rips apart the connecting tissue which causes people to live as neighbours, creates cultural superimpositions and grafts people together. None of this obscures the fact that, even at the practical level, we sometimes accomplish living together amid diverse identities and cultures. We are diversified and united, not only in the wider picture of globalization, but also in what has more affinity with us, our common interests, our neighbourhoods, our inter-breeding. This is a rich and complex experience, not easy to depict, but being lived out at this end of the 21st century.

This is a trend in history unforeseen at the end of the Second World War, or afterwards in the period of decolonization. It is a trend of history which we are not promised by Messianism, nor by pseudo-scientific thinking, nor by mechanistic Socialism. Tomorrow there could be earthquakes, but this trend of history is less obscure than it is often painted, providing we consent to look at it in all its complexity.

CHAPTER 3

BETWEEN CONFLICTS
AND CIVILIZATIONS

The ending of the European mission

Every day we are met by a huge mass of information and it is not easy to keep our bearings amid it all. We make hard work of organizing it. Most of us have no settled vision of the world. Perhaps we did have, when there was less information. Today, there is a thirst for some kind of orientation that will allow a better understanding of the interests of the group with which we identify, let us see where risks may be coming from for us, or simply let us know what is going on in other universes. In Italy, immediately after the end of the cold war, geopolitics took centre stage and with it a journal of geopolitics, *Limes*. This was symptomatic of the general public and not only the specialists asking for orientation.

How are we to explain what is happening in the great wide world beyond Europe and the West? During the nineteenth and twentieth centuries, colonialism had equipped many Europeans with their vision of the world. It was a vision sustained by the unspoken sense of superiority of our civilization and of the white race. This feeling was shared by many Europeans. Between 1853 and 1855, the theories of Arthur de Gobineau on the inequality of the human races considered whites to be superior in beauty, physical strength and intelligence, whilst blacks were held to be inferior and yellowed-skinned people limited. This theory much preoccupied Alexis de Tocqueville, who, nevertheless, was afraid that the spreading of it in Germany would become a collective obsession.

Between the nineteenth and twentieth centuries, no one doubted the superiority of whatever is white and European. At that time, human zoos were circulating in Europe. In 1853 a troupe of "kaffirs from Zululand" was organized in London and later went the rounds of Germany and France. The non-Europeans seemed ferocious and primitive. From 1877 to 1912, the *Jardin d'Acclimatation* in Paris organised a score of ethnological exhibitions using Africans, Indians, Eskimos and others. "Black Villages" were erected where the French could see primitive life in close up. This exhibiting of "examples" of other "savage" races popularized the idea of inequality.

In Paris, Malagasies were put on display a year after the French conquest of Madagascar. Colonial expansion was accompanied by keen involvement, deriving from consciousness of superiority and – in Kipling's words – the white man's burden.

In historical thinking, too little consideration has been given to colonialism as a relevant component in the self-consciousness of Europeans in their relations with the world. A modest sense of guilt accompanied decolonization and has endeavoured to find how best to close that particular dossier, and also how to avoid heavy compensation claims for colonial damages – like those submitted against Italy by Colonel Gaddafi. Yet colonialism speeded up the projection of important European countries on to the world scene, beginning with Great Britain and France, but also including Germany, Italy, Portugal, Holland and Belgium. A little more than a century ago, the world map, with its harmony of colours, showed the vast scale of the colonial phenomenon, with only the exception of the United States, Latin America and China. Although models of colonialism were very diverse, it etched itself deeply into national sentiment and its collective consciousness: on one side stood civilization and on the other "the barbarians".

From 1902, Great Britain celebrated Empire Day on the birthday of Queen Victoria to commemorate the unity of the Dominions, Colonies and the Indies around the royal crown. Colonial propaganda was spread by a network of societies. In the Hague in the Netherlands, out of about half a million inhabitants in 1940, around 60,000 had lived in the Dutch Indies, (today Indonesia). Until a few years ago, in old people's homes in Rome, one could still find a few Italians who came from very diverse places around the Mediterranean. The magnificent British Empire Exhibition was held in 1924 to celebrate the greatness of the Empire. The apotheosis of the colonial vision was the International Colonial Exhibition at Vincennes in France. Under the guiding hand of Marshal Lyautey, the great colonizer of Morocco and theoretician of France's Universal Mission, each colonial country had its own pavilion. Experience outside Europe left its mark on the lives of a steady stream of Europeans, and on the imagination of very many more. In wartime, the empires responded to the call of their mother country in its hour of danger. During the two world wars, Australians, New Zealanders, South Africans, Canadians and Indians fought with the British. Colonial troops were alongside the French. Mircea Eliade,the great historian of religions, tells of the amazement of his fellow Romanians, when they saw Bucharest being liberated in 1918 by "black" Senegalese troops marching beneath the French Tricoleur. In the great French military cemetery at Cassino, it is impressive how many Crescents there are, beside a lesser number of Crosses and Suns (an Animist symbol). The majority of the fallen came from the colonial empire, but all had "died for France", as the inscriptions attest.

The colonial period was also important in the formation of national European self-awareness. Victor Hugo, the great liberal-minded novelist, enthused over the French conquest of Algeria, asserting without a shadow of doubt, "Civilization is marching against barbarity. An enlightened people are going to seek out a people of darkness. We are the Greeks of the world; it is down to us to shed illumination in the world." Portugal under Salazar resisted decolonization for almost half the 1970s, although the country was strained to its limit, because "overseas" made up part of the vision of its historic mission. When it ended it seemed as if Portugal itself was finished.

Decolonization was inevitable, even for those who opposed it. The Americans and the Soviets, from their different perspectives, had no sympathy for colonial empires. The European countries had been weakened by the war. General de Gaulle, upholder of the grandeur of France, realised that the anti-colonial tidal wave was irresistible. Following their victory over Hitler, the English were unwilling to face up to a war for the defence of the Indian Empire. With all this happening, who would have gone to war over some strip of Africa? Perhaps it was not appropriate to maintain colonial rule. The vital interests of London could be guaranteed in other ways.

Decolonization was an enormous historic phenomenon at the heart of the twentieth century. The impact of it on European national self-awareness has been little studied, even though it was happening world wide. Such an event, completed over a few years, was more traumatic than one might think. It was little understood because it was believed that decolonization was both just and inevitable. The sense of superiority (not only racial) with which Europeans used to regard the world during the nineteenth and twentieth centuries, was wrecked by two world wars, by the emergence of the United States, by new visions for the world asserting themselves, by a culture of equality, by decolonization... A new geopolitical vision had emerged after the Second World

War; this was the epoch-making confrontation of civilization and power of the West and the Soviet empire. The cold war obscured the repercussions of the end of the colonial empires and it hid its traumatic impact on the countries of Europe. The ex-colonial countries fitted themselves into the Western camp, alongside the United States. They still kept an international function, even if their capacity for political and military intervention was reduced. But, from the ending of their colonies, European countries were no longer what they used to be. The West became something more than an empire, despite the political and military primacy of the United States. It was a cohesive yet plural world order. There was room for the autonomous France of de Gaulle, for the faith-based nations such as Italy, for special relationships such as the Anglo-American, for the Catholic Church of Pius XII, for a pro-Western left wing, for a right wing, for Christian Democrats, for Salazar's Portugal. However, the opposite, the Soviet camp was organized as an imperial unit under political-military control which stretched over a very precisely known territory, even if there was no lack of schisms such as Yugoslavia and the Albanian-Chinese relationship.

In those days, the geo-political map was clear; today it no longer is.

A new map of civilizations with ancient roots

The world since 1989 has lacked any map of political orientations. With the ending of the cold war (and we can all too easily forget the climate of tension and the atomic threat that coloured some moments of that), people believed that an era of great peace would begin. But it has not happened. People believed that 1989 would lead to the universalization of the principles of liberty and democratic methods of government.

This was the basic theme of Francis Fukuyama, who talked of the end of history as the universalization of democracy and liberty, and of the market economy as the focus of political and international life. Here was the universal victory of Western democracy. This thesis has been refuted by fifteen successive years, when there has been no lack of clashes and conflicts.

The cold war allowed us a simple, effective bipolar vision. Opposition between East and West is an historical commonplace. It had never been as simple, as it became during the post-second war period, to recognize "the East"; it had fortified borders and an ideology to refer to. From the 1990s onwards, everything has become confused, for decision-makers in world politics, for ruling classes and also for the people who read the newspapers.

In 1993, Samuel Huntington put forward a proposal in an article called "The Clash of Civilizations" published in *Foreign Affairs* and in a following volume. He suggested some conceptual tools for tracing out a map of the world, not limited by political or legal boundaries, but paying attention to matters that denote cultures and civilizations. According to this American scholar, the great watersheds of history were not the frontiers of states, but the entirety of countries and civilizations, which are cultural and religious entities. It was becoming easier to locate a national identity from looking into a civilization. In the time of the cold war, countries used to be asked, "Which side are you on?" Today the question is, "Who are you?", which is not easy to answer, for there is so much to be said about the reconstruction process that is happening to every identity.

The civilizations cited by Huntington are naturally the Western (the strongest), plus the Islamic, the Chinese, the Indian, the Orthodox, the Buddhist, the Japanese and the African. In the course of his discussion, some civilizations are given a high profile, whilst others – especially the

African – are marginalized, almost casting doubt on their coherence. The American scholar has the merit of putting forward an order of classification in a "dust-storm" of identities that have revived or are already very much alive. He includes a map for readers to use. In his interpretation, civilization, cultures, and religions regain the value that they lost in the years of the cold war and through Marxist analyses. Being critical of the idea that globalization tends towards a universal civilization, Huntington maintains that it is merely a coating that hides the great variety of the peoples of the world.

There is one globalized and cosmopolitan culture, which the author calls the "Davos culture" (after the Swiss centre that is famous for its meetings of top people), but it involves only a few. According to Huntington, "Davos culture" manages to embrace no more than fifty million or so people outside the Western world. Popular global culture has shallow roots and is not a tool for unification. The same goes for the use of English as a lingua franca. In fact, we are in a phase of re-using local languages, as we can see from the former USSR and several African countries, where local languages are being re-advocated as a medium for recovering people's true identity. Globalization does not create a single world civilization; it is only a thin crust, beneath which radically different societies live on.

Huntington's thesis has been popularised as the "Clash of Civilizations" (except that, in the Italian edition, the second part of the title "Remaking of World Order" is given a much higher profile). The book's value lies in its affirmation of the strength of the long-term factors, such as culture, the civil community and religion. Some, especially those who have not read him, reduce Huntington to being the prophet of the clash of civilizations. Yet he is much more than that. Besides, the key-stone of this interpretation, civilization, is not an invention by that author but has healthy roots in historiographical tradition.

The international profile of the USSR was a continuation of the Russian-Tsarist and the dynamics of the Third Rome continued to operate after the break-up caused by the Bolshevik revolution. Huntington is not proposing some novelty when he talks about a clash of civilizations. The cold war had simply hidden the constant strength of civilizations from most people's eyes.

In the 1930s, a French Catholic organization for discussing society, called *Semaines Sociales*, held a session devoted to the conflicts between civilizations and identified several, including Islamic, Soviet and Jewish. Their thesis was that Christianity transcended civilizations as a force for peace. It is significant that French Catholicism in the 1930s was already aware of the impact of other worlds and cultures and was thinking about civilizations and the clash between them, even in an epoch in which people were assuming a "white" hegemony. In addition, an English Protestant writer, Basil Matthews, published a book in 1925 called *Young Islam on Trek* and subtitled it *A Study in the Clash of Civilizations*, aiming to encourage young Christians to reflect on the confrontation between the Christian and the Islamic worlds.

What is more, at the very end of the 1930s, the Vatican undertook an enquiry among Catholic bishops in Muslim countries to find out what might be done when confronted by an Islam which could not be penetrated by Catholic missionary work. There was intense debate and the responses coalesced around a consensus for living respectfully alongside each other. The Islamic world, its resistance and its strength were well known in the West, so much so that there was thinking about conflict between civilizations at a time when almost all the Islamic countries were living under European control.

Thus, Huntington's book has behind it a rich cultural tradition. We need only think of *Sunset of the West* by Oswald Spengler, which was a reference point used by our American author. It was published after the First World War and makes ample use of the category of civilizations, noting their points of distress. The historian Arnold Toynbee also reflected on the relationship of the West with other civilizations.

The moment at which Huntington published his analysis was a time which greatly felt the need of some orientation. Many people wanted to hear what he had to say. These people were the orphans of the struggle against Communism who were seeking a new enemy and new barbarians from whom to defend themselves. Added to that, the Slav-Russian world was feeling itself diminished by the collapse of the USSR, by the war in Yugoslavia (with which the Serbs identified) and by being subjected to Western pressure. One orientation on offer was for a world that was purely Islamic. There was also an interest in the Hindu orientation. The conflict of civilizations offered a place where restless souls could find their niche, tempted by its alternative opposing vision. It is no accident that Huntington's book became a best-seller among Arabs, especially the Islamists, who felt confirmed in their opinion that the West should be resolutely opposed. So the book was a success even among the "enemies" of the West.

Many conflicts but what kind of civilization?

The world is still in conflict after 1989. According to the Human Security Centre, there has, since 1992, been a notable reduction in conflicts, although even more civilians have been killed than in the past. However, Africa is an exception to this lessening of warfare. Many of the conflicts were not exclusively rooted in confrontation between the two superpowers, as some used to maintain. The empires used to restrict conflict situations. This fact has been made clear since the collapse of the USSR, at which several wars broke out: in Chechnya, in

Nagorny-Karabakh (in Azerbaijan) and in South Ossetia in Georgia, which was demanding reunification with Russia, and there are still more areas. Several wars that were considered to be conflicts-by-proxy between the two empires, had local root-causes. For example, it is true that, since 1989, the revolutionary movements in Central America had lost their external support, and even Cuba was weakened as Soviet aid faded away. However, the fighting in Colombia has not ended, where Marxist movements play a big role. The Islamic war (supported by the West) against the Soviets in Afghanistan was a decisive episode in awakening the aggressive forces of radical Islamism. In Algeria, there were former fighters in Afghanistan, who now had their own base in a mosque in Algiers which had once been a Catholic church, and they reinvented themselves as terrorists. The historic Israel-Palestine conflict has lasted more than half a century and is still going along its painful way, despite calming down at some stages, such as that following the Oslo negotiations. The seemingly miraculous détente between one part of the Arab world (Egypt under Sadat) and Israel happened in the time of the cold war.

Countless perils remain, partly because of the growing distribution of increasingly deadly weapons. Using these, people can enter into armed struggle. The ability to make war is now possible for so many people. Our world remains in conflict, but not all the conflicts are to do with civilizations; many have their basis in local situations, in endemic political crises (as in Colombia), in the difficulties of living together. Terrorism does not only happen in the guise of the encounter between Islam and the West. The Kurdish PKK's fight against Turkey is not of that sort. Even if Western targets, especially tourists are attacked in that country, the aim is to weaken the government in Ankara. Conflict runs through the Islamic world itself: radicals against the "impious" powers who do not practise theocracy. Powerful conflicts between Shiites and Sunnis snake their way through Iraq and Pakistan. The attack of 31 August 2005 in Baghdad against the Shiite faithful gathered at the Mosque of Musa al Kasim was carried out by an armed Sunni group considered to be close to Al Qaeda. These are events occurring around an Islamic-Islamic clash; it is not a clash of civilizations.

The world has become globalized but not unified. Globalization has brought about new systems of communication, technologies, and commercial and cultural products. It has brought remote places closer together. It has not given birth to any general respect for rights and values. The People's Republic of China does not allow similar human rights to those enjoyed in the West, nor does it have a democratic system. But it has opened up to capitalism, while holding strictly to the one-party political system of its Communist history. A good number of the Islamic countries do not recognize human rights as ratified in international circles; indeed, the Cairo conference in 1990 subordinated human rights to Sharia law. Actions by the United Nations have met with big impediments to do with this. There are still frontiers that are hard to cross; there are still social groups where it is not easy to intervene. We observe the caution of western countries over human rights in China. The question of the death penalty divides European countries from the United States.

Some alternative cultural universes are being designed to contrast with the Western hegemony. The boundaries of civilizations are under discussion. There are worlds and areas that overlap. People discuss whether Latin America is a civilization in itself, distinct from North America and Europe. For example, Argentina is a "distant Europe". Yet we are seeing a rise of anti-Americanism and indigenous ideology in Latin America which is reshaping the political life not only of Venezuela under Hugo Chavez, but also in Bolivia under Evo

Morales (an indigenous ex-cocaine farmer). By means of these developments and through electoral processes, Latin-American society is re-thinking itself in a way that is over and against the United States. Can one have a debate over the boundaries of the West (Western Europe and the United States?) with Latin America? Civilizations do not have sharp and certain boundaries like states – their individuality depends on many motives and many criteria. However, they really do exist and we are meeting them all the time.

The world remains divided, strongly divided. It remains divided among civilizations. It remains divided between the great powers, such as the United States, Russia, China, India, Europe, and Japan. On the Asiatic scene, China and India are growing larger as countries and civilizations with their own strength, great histories and a position of growing importance awaiting them in the future. It is not only a question of demography, even though that is centre-stage and very influential, but it is also to do with their economy, culture, political power and the forward thrust that enlivens those societies. We must ask ourselves about the long-term effect of Chinese demographic pressure on Siberia, which is sparsely inhabited and rich in resources and in a Russia with a steep fall in its population. Yet for all that, Russia, with all its weaknesses, is still the heart of a Slav whole that cannot be left out of account.

North American policy, even if it has decided to press for its objectives in some regions of the world, like Iraq, is showing itself to be very soft in other places, attentively taking account of others' susceptibilities, mostly because it is not able to manage an immense number of questions and crises on its own. For instance, I have noticed how, in some African crises, United States policy is very respectful of local spokespersons, despite its disproportionate strength. This is a consequence of the super-power not being able to be involved everywhere. Sometimes, it needs the help of others, even in small countries.

It is not easy for the Europeans to understand the United States, since they have lost the parameters of cold war without finding any others to use. The clear "fraternity" of sharing a common enemy with the Americans during the cold war has been diluted in a world which is so much larger. The American West has an internal complexity which baffles Europeans. America has its imperial functions, but the call to lead a single world empire is impractical in a world with so very many subjects, some of whom are very powerful and some are very unruly. The structure of the contemporary world is multi-polar. This has not been chosen nor is it a problem deriving from international politics but simply a reality, anchored deep in the heartlands of the civilizations. Maybe the world has always been multi-polar, but it is only today that this reality is now clearly manifest. A plethora of interventions cannot cancel out the diversities and the pluralities of the potential subjects, some of whom are very strong. The United States is rethinking itself, but it is not fading away. The most notable example is the European Union which, despite recent difficulties, has proved capable of holding medium and small European countries in association (there are no large countries, despite France and Great Britain having seats in the Security Council of the United Nations Organization). The international profile of the Union is a challenge to be met in future. The EU has transformed relationships between European countries, but will it ever go any further?

In a world without unity, battered by the winds of disorientation, a good number of states feel the need to be linked to others, even if they do not follow this up completely. States do not die even if they are fragile, because they express the identity of a people and a ruling class. On the contrary, states are multiplying on the world scene, as they did during decolonization and the ending of the USSR. But they are well aware of their fragility and feel the need of systems in which they can locate themselves. These systems are harmonizing different states and overcoming historic rivalries. We have seen, and we shall see, epoch-making changes, such as the twentieth century rapprochement between France and Germany, whose conflicts had been at the epicentre of two world wars. But in Latin America too, as I have pointed out, a new kind of cohesion is being tested out, anti-American in function and done in the name of pride in their own autonomy.

This discussion is not only about states. Some years ago, a great deal was spoken about civil society, which is a useful but fluid expression, and can sometimes be a mythical refuge when no other solution can be found. Nevertheless, civil society does exist; there are societies and transnational groupings, there are communities and shared interests that go beyond frontiers. To sum up, we are discussing the grouping together of diverse peoples on the national and the international scene. Account must be taken of them. Indeed, peace and living together are not a choice for leaders of states alone. They involve all the people. This is not just a good, democratically inspired thought, but is a reality which must be attended to. Today, with the potential of the firearms that are in circulation, so many people have the capacity to destabilize a region or a state by making war. The Internet spreads their message. Just consider Chiapas and the actions of Sub-commandant Marcos, who communicated with the world from a remote corner of Mexico, until, by 1994, he had risen to a fame of mythical proportions.

On the other hand, people can work for peace in small ways. The experience of the Community of Sant'Egidio in Mozambique and other African countries has been to assume the role of mediator. In the case of Mozambique, Sant'Egidio sponsored a negotiation, with Italian and American support, which put an end to a war that had caused a million deaths and lasted for more than ten years, even though it was out of the spotlight of public opinion. There are civil, national or transnational agencies in the world for bringing about a more serene living together. Moreover, according to the Human Security Centre, the development of active mediation and prevention is a fundamental component in bringing a reduction in the recourse to war. We should look to the great religions which involve millions of people: without losing the original character of their faith (although there are differences among them), they can be a deep influence in civil life and for peace.

Religions have become important again. This has been noticed even by the culture which had devalued their role and considered their end as an inevitable outcome of international modernity. It was thought that, after Europe, secularization would have overwhelmed even the most "backward" societies. It has not happened and, over the last twenty years, we have witnessed a growing public role for the religions, not only Islam, but also Judaism, Hinduism, and Christianity. The pontificate of John Paul II has illustrated the strength of Roman Catholicism, in, for example, the emancipation of Poland from the Soviet bloc. The non-violent but effective role of Solidarity cannot be explained without the support of the Catholic Church which became a space for an alternative civil society to Communism in Poland.

Globalization has had a powerful impact on the religions. Fundamentalist Islam has spread itself by using the apparatus of globalization. But this has not unified the world from a religious point of view. There has been no rise of the universal religion proposed by scholars of the religions in 1900 at the beginning of last century, during a great congress in Paris, which picked out the elements that are common to the various religions. Even the attempt to create a universal ethic is on the ropes, because it was the fruit of laboratory research. Nor, despite some attempts, will there be a United Nations

Organization of the religions. They cannot be reduced to a common denominator. Notwithstanding the growth of dialogue, the religions persist with their substantial differences in theology, in relations with society, in the way of life they teach. And sometimes we are seeing the rebirth of old conflicts.

The map of religions, with their irreducible differences, demonstrates how our globalized world remains in its diversity. Does a "Globalized Balkanization" exist? Must diversity necessarily lead to conflict? In order to be at peace, must the world aspire to being unified and homogenised in depth, like some single great nation-state? Like it or not, this project will not work. The contemporary world does not function in that way. However, diversity need not mean violent conflict. We need to live together: in the same environment, among our neighbours and among people far away. Terror can certainly come from far away, as happened in New York in 2001. How can we try to live in peace, even with those who are far away?

We must found a civilization of living together among very many elements in our world: states, religions, economic realities, cultures, civil societies… We must found this civilization if we want a future that is peaceful. Such a civilization does already exist in many regions; it is written into the chromosomes of the religions and into the disposition of their cultures. The civilization of living together already exists in part, but we need to enlarge it, make it stable, and increase the consensus of the people about its rightness. An immense cultural work remains to be done, if this is to be achieved. Culture is becoming important again. We must discuss and negotiate with all the interested parties. To achieve this work of broadening minds, we need an articulate vision of the world, illuminated by the realization that we need to live together. The civilization of living together is no utopian model but is a present partial reality, even if we are always in need of more hard work to continue to construct a life together, at many levels, as this is the condition for having a peaceful future or, at least, a future with fewer conflicts.

CHAPTER 4
EURAFRICA

Where does Africa's future lie?

Where does Africa stand today? From a study of Huntington's maps of civilizations, we can find a faint trace of Africa as a civilization in itself, but, as we go through the pages of the book, the idea becomes lost. Africa, at least the part of it south of the Sahara, is not part of Islamic civilization, even if it is a territory where Islam is expanding. White Africa, above the Sahara, belongs to the Arab world. So, where does Africa stand today? It is a question to reflect on for the sake of the continent's future.

Relationships between European countries and Africa are complicated; the shadow of colonialism hangs heavy. *The Black Book of Colonialism* (an analysis of its crimes) points out many, many tragic aspects of the time when some of the European powers controlled, exploited and governed Africa. Europeans boasted about their role as bringers of civilization, but today it is clear that things were not like that. We need only recall the ethnic cleansings committed by colonialism, among them the genocide perpetrated by the Germans in Namibia. Generally speaking, there has been too little progress in understanding the history of colonialism. Even though tragic, it is still a story that Europe and Africa share together and it has left its imprint.

When they are faced with difficulties, African leaders often invoke the heavy burden left by colonialism. They have right on their side, but African countries have been (more or less) independent for almost half a century and the current problems of Africa are not all inherited from colonialism. Europeans hover between flushes of arrogance and the fear of appearing colonialist. People rarely take the trouble to reflect on Africa and seek to create a new atmosphere which takes account of the shared heritage. Colonialism is a "comfortable" story, despite its uncomfortable aspect for both sides but to think in this way can prevent realism about the present day.

In the middle of the Second World War, Simone Weil explained French colonialism with immense clarity by comparing it with Nazism which was seeking to colonize Europe. That meant depriving the nations of their soul and reducing them "to the state of human matter". Those words throw light on a disturbing experience, yet it still remains a fact of history with all its many tragic, destructive and harsh aspects. In any case, many, many parts of human history are all too similar. The painful colonial experience has left Africa a changed place. This is not only a question of blame and merit, this is simply being realistic. Colonial history has created a powerful bond between Europe and Africa, involving languages, political and mental attitudes, emigration, culture, exchanges, sometimes producing genuinely cross-bred cultures. It has been a history lived out by two profoundly unequal partners. This must never happen again, and yet Europe and Africa still possess so much in common.

However, nothing in history can be taken for granted. Some European countries are settling down quietly to the fact that Africa is mostly ending up in the European orbit. Some are hypersensitive to being erstwhile colonialists, like France when it is faced with the presence of America or perhaps a feared reduction in the dissemination of the French language. After the end of the cold war, with Russia far away and no longer a rival, Africa has come to be considered as western by nature. This has not increased the commitment of the

European countries. This has even declined. But during the most recent years, policies for co-operation and help with development have greatly increased. The marginal situation of Africa compared with the emerging nations highlights the deeply impoverished condition of the continent. Africa has many problems from which the European countries have learned to stay well away. Deep down, they would like to "purify" Europe from its proximity to a dangerously infectious instability.

The 1990s began with a forceful military operation in Africa. This was the expedition into Somalia, which was undergoing a humanitarian crisis and the violence of the warlords. Bush senior had wanted it and Clinton continued it. The Italians took part alongside the Americans and others. The beginning took place under spotlights, but the operation became bogged down in the super-hot climate and because of fighting among the Somalis. It demanded too high a price in human lives and ended in retreat. Somalia has never returned to being a state but has remained a land for warlords. The failure was understandable because of the difficulty of making the intervention. Nevertheless, there has been too little consideration that the Somalia event may be significant well beyond Somalia itself. African – and Islamic – consciousness has perceived this defeat of Westerners as an important event, whilst in our own countries it is forgotten. Significantly, Osama bin Laden emphasizes the weakness of American soldiers, judging them like this, "They forgot about being the leaders of the world, and the guides of the new world order. They went away with their dead and the shame of defeat behind them."

Osama's manuals on Italian history recall the defeat at Adua in 1896 at the hands of the Ethiopians. He is putting out a message to the African world, "The Europeans are not invincible." Something similar happened with Somalia; here the fundamentalists interpreted humanitarian intervention as an aggression against Islamic territory so grievous that it provoked Afghan veterans into taking part in attacks causing the death of eighteen United States military personnel. The United States attributed responsibility for the killings to bin Laden's men. Western diplomatic corps also drew a lesson from the Somalia experience which was that intervention in Africa is not easy because of the nature of the conflicts and the cost in human lives involved. It is not easy to win wars in Africa but the greatest difficulty is to build the peace. The 1994 intervention by America and France in Rwanda – a genocide which claimed 800,000 victims – demonstrated the difficulty in coming out of the African quagmire with any dignity. The same can be seen with the French intervention in Ivory Coast (a land divided in two, between a Christian nation in the south and a Muslim north).

A drifting Africa is dangerous for Africa, but it is also dangerous for the world and especially for its neighbour Europe. Africa is a land of much hopelessness, where people see their life-expectancy growing shorter. They talk of war but they think of AIDS. There are thirty million people infected with HIV-AIDS, and, for the most part, their problem has only been tackled by preventive measures. Drugs to cure AIDS have been available since 1996. But drugs cost money and so people have preferred to concentrate on the easier campaign of prevention, even when it is known that no epidemic has ever been beaten solely by prevention. The prevention campaign has been a large-scale failure. For example, in Mozambique they speak of about 30% of the population being infected.

How can any African accept death or see their own children die, when this disease can be cured in other parts of the world? Yet the Africans are too poor and too marginalized to have access to those cures. This is just one aspect of the drama of being excluded in a world where people are able to see what is happening far away and can know that a cure is possible. The explosive potential of such desperation must not be underestimated. It is said that terrorism is practised by youngsters trained and turned into fanatics, and not by the desperately poor. True enough. But Africans, trained or not, but certainly desperate, constitute a reserve, a useful work-force for whoever wishes to weave subversive conspiracies. The Americans have taken notice and have registered "a net increase in the strategic importance" of Africa in the fight against Islamic terrorism, along with a significant financial and military investment. A high-ranking American official has declared that the terrorists "are looking for places where chaos and illegal activities reign, where there is no control exercised by government".

The response to desperation

Desperation is fertile ground for those seeking vocations to radicalism. It is no accident that, in 1998, the first terrorist appearance of the Islamic International Front against Jews and Crusaders (founded by bin Laden with Ayman al Zawahiri as a member) was in Africa with attacks that destroyed the American Embassies in Dar es Salaam and Nairobi, causing 11 and 213 deaths respectively. On the other hand, the empty spaces and the fragility of the African states produce an opportunity for anyone seeking space in which to set up networks and command centres. In a fragile and poverty-stricken state in southern Africa, Malawi (population 12 million), the development of fundamentalist groups has been noted among the Muslim minority (about 1.8% of the population). Malawi is a country where one can clearly discern the desperation of African life. Between 2000 and the present time, life expectancy has fallen again from 40 to 36 years. Of every 100 babies, 11 are born with AIDS. There are recurrent famines among people who live by farming and their principal implement is still the hoe. I visited Malawi in 2004 and spoke with some young people. Hard questions kept recurring, "Why are we inflicted with AIDS?" "What hopes do we have for the future?" These questions remain unanswered.

I thought of these questions again in 2005, when I heard that five non-Malawian Muslims with links to terrorism had been arrested in Malawi. The event provoked a revolt by the local Muslims in the fundamentalist stronghold with attacks on foreign non-governmental organizations and the burning down of four churches. Perhaps fundamentalism has started to answer the questions of those young people in its own way. These are episodes which show how subversive networks can be set up on African soil, thanks to the fragility of governmental institutions and widespread desperation among the people. These facts indicate how radical Islam may be able to offer itself to Africans in the guise of a liberation ideology. This may become a false but exciting answer to the questions of those young people who were asking about their future.

On the road to independence Africa drank at the wells of liberationist Marxism. There it discovered several answers and keywords. For many governments, Marxism was the grammar of politics (preferably with a tang of anti-Westernism, which was not breaking down after the end of colonialism). Marxism gave dreams of rapidly winning a decent life without going down the road of Western capitalism. It offered "scientific" guarantees for the future. It hid the madness of some dictatorships. On the other hand, it provided an ethic for the use of the ruling groups and a language for communication between them and the people.

All that is now finished. And many are still left empty. Will a policy of Islamization now put itself forward as the ideological instrument to express a revolt against marginalization?

African Islam has its own strong characteristics which are resistant to the new attitudes now flowing through the Muslim world. In the Ivory Coast, I heard an authoritative imam (who is not pro-government) speak positively about the secular nature of the state. Coming from a Muslim, that is amazing. This fraternal temperament in African Islam is part of a resistance to radicalism. However, we must not underestimate the unhealthy effects of the Saudi enterprise, which is teaching Wahabita, religious rigourism, and is having a powerful impact on the younger generations. These same young people are then applying this rigourism even to their Saudi benefactors. (That kind of story repeats itself in very many parts of the world.) I do not mean to exaggerate the dangers, but the battle is on – outside politics – to win control of the ideals and values of very many parts of Africa.

Some states have finished up in the hands of groups from the criminal fringes. That was the story in Liberia, an African country with a great history which was created by the return of freed American slaves. Later, however, it was governed by the clan of Charles Taylor with obvious criminal connections. There are states which could finish up in the hands of Mafias or subversive cliques. Some are so weak that criminal money can easily take power, even from an economic point of view. Bin Laden conducted a similar operation in Afghanistan, adopted as his base and protected by the impassable borders of the country, after Sudanese hospitality became impractical. His people found space for themselves in Somalia and in lawless areas of Pakistan. Fragile states can be attracted by this or just offer no resistance to the pressures of terrorism or international crime.

There are regions outside anyone's control. Consider the great, rich land of the Congo, which went successively through dark years under Mobutu and then hard years of warfare from 1997 to 2002. Three million citizens were killed, only 6% of them dying in battle: that is more than died during the forty years of cold war in Africa. In several regions the Congolese state was stripped to pieces and finished up under the control of various political groups.

To sum up, there is always some African giant at risk of being made like Somalia whose great natural resources, often exploited in "unofficial" ways, are nowadays of little interest to international commerce. We could go back to the old cartography which used to write on maps *terrae incognitae* to designate regions that were outside the reach of control, and also *hic sunt leones* to indicate dangers. Today's problems come, not from the lions but from "wild beasts" of another sort.

There is a strong link between war and poverty. First and foremost war is the "mother of all forms of poverty": it impoverishes, it leaves an inheritance of poverty which slowly resolves itself over time. From a statistical point of view, the 32 poorest countries in the world are those most exposed to conflicts. A good 22 of these – mostly African – have suffered warfare between 1990 and today. Some others – although affected by war – cannot be compared statistically for lack of reliable data. An Africa in crisis creates grave problems beyond the borders of the continent. We live together in the contemporary world, distances are shortening and instability is spreading.

The avalanche of emigration

It is neither wise nor prudent that there should be vast regions of hopelessness and poverty, almost on the frontiers of the wealthy European world. It is a delusion to think that the crisis of Africa leaves Europe unscathed. That is to undervalue the world's intercommunication and the porous nature of its frontiers. We must ask ourselves, "In what way can the crises in the Congo or in Burundi produce fall-out over Europe?" They will do so, and not only on some European economic interests in Africa, but as a contagion that will come in the long term and at long distance from its source. The constant emigration arriving on the coasts of Europe is a clear piece of evidence for this. It is true that this emigration is not only from Africa, but, in the African imagination, Europe is a desirable landing place. A world is pushing at our door. As the great French historian Jean-Baptiste Duroselle wrote, this type of emigration is an "invasion". And invasions do not stop at frontiers.

The Spanish are observing this as they see an "avalanche" of Africans pouring into Ceuta and Melilla, its national territories on the Moroccan coast. Not even mantraps and severe measures are able to block it. In 2003, around Ceuta and Melilla, Moroccan soldiers arrested 25,000 Africans, of whom 12,400 came from Morocco. In 2005, the proportion of Africans increased among the immigrants pressing to get in. In 2004, 13,620 illegal immigrants landed on the coasts of Sicily. This was the same number as in the previous year, thus demonstrating a continuing trend. The Maltese authorities have calculated that almost 600 migrants die in shipwrecks in the Mediterranean and that is 4.41% of the numbers who reached Sicily. Since 1966, there have been 6,356 confirmed victims. However, according to research by one English university, deaths run at about 2,000 in each year. Many of the immigrants have set out from deep inside Africa and have passed through incredible hazards. No network or police force will stop them, unless death has blocked their way along the road! Must weapons be used against them on the very soil of Europe?

These people are fleeing from the profound crisis that grips Africa. Since 2002, the crisis in the Ivory Coast has thrown four million people on to the streets; in Liberia, a good three million have gone the same way. This is the effect of the

93

attraction of better living standards and the myths about Europe. I recall being told by a young man from the Ivory Coast who was on his first visit to Paris, "At last I have seen my stepmother." Thousands and thousands of Africans – especially the young – have a fantasy that Europe is the ideal life to reach out for. They are attempting to make the journey from the most unlikely and remote places. Their journeys are always difficult: they cross the desert, they are in the hands of unscrupulous mercenaries, they sail the seas in small boats. No matter: young and desperate, they take risks. Sometimes it is a game of chance, "suicidal heroism". One immigrant who made it to the shores of Italy declared that his aim had been to get there and "Only death could have stopped us. And we asked no one for help, before Malta."

In 1999, two young men from Guinea Conakry, Yaguine and Fode, were found frozen to death in the undercarriage of an aircraft which landed at Brussels having taken off from their home country. Unlike many dead immigrants in similar circumstances, they had left a message. Their naïve hope had been to find a country where young people could live well. Their desperation cried out, "… we appeal to your comradeship and kindness to come to Africa's aid. Help us, we are suffering horribly in Africa; help us, we have problems and the little children have no human rights. Our problems are war, sickness, food and so it goes on…" Their desire had been to make a respectful request to the "Ladies and Gentlemen of Europe". "We beg you to create a great and effective organization so that Africa can make progress." These two boys (15 and 14 years old) wrote, "So, if you see us risking our lives, it is because we are suffering too much in Africa, we need you to fight this poverty and put an end to war in Africa." They had been aware of the risks in their journey but they had put their hopes in a future that would hold the same possibilities as those enjoyed by Europeans, "We want to study and we ask you to help us study so that we can be like you in Africa."

To be like you in Africa? Behind African "pride", there is a great longing to live like Europeans and with their standards of well-being. That desire is the passion that produces so many journeys of hope. Guinea was the country which refused to be integrated into the French-African community proposed by General de Gaulle. It went through the long dictatorship of Sekou Toure, with its socialistic terror and isolationism. The dream of a new Guinean Man was wrecked amid violence, with at least 50,000 people murdered. The great Ivory Coast novelist Ahmadou Kourouma wrote bitterly, "Everything except the torture chamber lay in ruins like a leper's hut." The regime finished in 1984 when the dictator died: the problems have not finished.

Other stories from Africa are not all as gloomy as that of Guinea. There are some, even many positive aspects. Yet, behind the emigration from Africa, there lies a story of suffering and disappointment for everyone. At the time of decolonization the people believed in the historic destiny of their own countries. Fourteen states became free in 1960, containing 120 million citizens. This was the introduction into politics for millions of women and men filled with passionate nationalism. For the most part, this world is over and gone. Kourouma admitted in his 1970 novel *Les soleils des independences* (a significant text about the turn taken by African culture), "at the time, we were naively thinking that these independences would fix all our problems".

This was not to be the case. The tide of emigration tells us that; it is the search for another world for self and family, a choice which is born from seeing television images of European wealth. This vision ripens among the young unemployed in the cities, who often have a measure of education and are looking for salvation and freedom from poverty and backwardness and seeking to turn over a new page in their style of living. The crisis of Africa is seeking new outlets in the old continent. The Africans are turning to the Europeans. Is it even thinkable that any kind of screening can hold them back? I believe not and, what is more, the countries of Europe need immigrants. A cross-bred Euro-African culture already exists in many European cities. Major difficulties confront Moroccan immigrants in becoming integrated into Europe. The problems of Africa are not being solved by emigration.

For the sake of completeness, it has to be said that the remittances sent home by emigrants have become a source of great relief, greater than in the past. In 2000 – according to the International Monetary Fund – these remittances reached 100 million dollars, overtaking public forms of help and representing one half of direct external monetary investment. Their spreading, drop by drop, and its management by families is having a very productive impact, because it avoids bureaucracy and corruption. This is the fruit of the 175 million working people in the world who have moved from their own country but continue to support it out of their income. Emigrants have become relief-donors for the development of their own land. We are not only speaking of temporary emigration but of a stable long-term relocation, yet one which does not interrupt links with the country of origin. This is one of the networks that binds Europe to Africa.

But 20 million immigrants into Europe are not going to change the predicament of the African continent. To be concerned with Africa is an expression of solidarity: it would be unseemly not to be, since the imbalance of resources is so great between North and South. To be concerned about Africa simply fits in with the interests of European countries. The crisis of Africa will unload itself on to Europe. A huge number of armaments is circulating around the dark continent. The times are long past when the world's poor were isolated and unaware of what was happening elsewhere. Could it not be one day that a Che Guevara or a bin Laden will emerge from the dangerous currents now flowing and take charge not only of the exasperation and desperation but also of the human strength that comes from having no future?

I am still impressed by having once seen young Africans putting on T-shirts with the effigy bin Laden on them without really knowing what he stands for. I received no clear answer when I asked about the terrorist. It was a fashion, a symbol of an indistinct desire to be different. Someone had provided those T-shirts. When people are looking for an alternative and are not finding it, they will use whatever symbols they have at their disposal. What is more, some buses in Bolivia display the image of the Saudi terrorist beside that of Che. Visiting African countries and having contact with young Africans has made me feel both the risks and the inherent potential of their continent. In the marginalized parts of the world, can we not foresee a violent protest by the excluded youth which is now, today, reaching the margins of urban Europe? Africa will be an increasingly young continent compared with a Europe of grey heads. In history, population growth is often accompanied by powerful subversive forces. Even if they are excluded, groups of humans can make themselves felt in our world, albeit by giving pain to others.

A Eurafrican vision of the future

Africa is not "all black", so Lucio Caracciolo entitled an issue of his review dedicated to that continent. Stable countries, such as South Africa, exercise the role of regional powers. Present-day Uganda is a strong country, yet its north, on the border with the Sudan, is tormented by ethnic guerrillas and

Christian fundamentalists who are guided by some mysterious personage. There, the war has forced one and a half million people to leave their homes. There are countries which have not experienced traumatic events, such as Kenya, Tanzania and Senegal. The last named country, with an overwhelming Muslim majority (94% of 11 million inhabitants), is a model of living together by Christian and Muslims, despite the native and confraternal character of its Islam. Nigeria, the seventh largest producer of petroleum products in the world, is shaken by several internal problems (among them conflict between Muslims and Christians) but remains a power to be reckoned with. And so would the Congo, were it not held back by its long-term crisis.

One medium-small country can tell its own special story of rebirth. I am not mentioning it because I played a part in this, but because I think it is symbolic. I speak of Mozambique. The country became independent from Portugal in 1975, following a painful war of liberation which was followed by the installation of a collectivist regime. Over the following years and until 1992, a grave civil war claimed a million deaths. I speak from direct experience because, through the Community of Sant' Egidio, I, with Matteo Zuppi, was mediator in the peace process between the government (Marxist) and the guerrillas. Civil war had devastated the country, reduced it to famine, deprived it of administrative structures and caused a proven serious degeneration of its civil society. The market in the capital, Maputo, had no food for sale except a little dry fish and a small amount of vegetables. It was the very image of general misery.

Since the peace was signed in Rome in 1992, that very poor country has experienced democracy with three successive terms of presidential elections (all won by the ex-Marxist party against the candidature of the ex-leader of the guerrillas). Mozambique has had economic development and is now concentrating on the cure of AIDS – thanks especially to the "Dream" programme of Sant'Egidio. This is a story of civil peace regained. It is also a story of economic development (with a rapid transition from collectivism to a free market economy) and also a story of collaboration between Europeans and Africa at many levels and between Africans too.

Ten years ago, whilst Europe was absorbed with the East, in chancelleries and international centres they used to repeat the slogan, "Africa for the Africans". This dictum was being faithful to the Monroe doctrine which excluded every non-American intervention in Latin America. The Monroe doctrine aimed to warn Europeans that the American continent was the exclusive reserve of the United States. For Africa it has a different meaning. It was not exclusive reserve that people wanted but freedom and the absence of politically biased investment sheltering behind political correctness. Despite the extinguishing of its imperial vision, some would say that Europe does not know how to think out its presence in Africa in a fresh way. Third world solidarity has been extinguished. Co-operation over development is mired in difficulties over balances of payments. The rich countries are spending little in Africa, only about 0.25% of their gross national product: the USA 0.16%, Japan 0.19%. In 2004 Italy offered public aid for development amounting to only 0.15% of gross national product, thus slipping to tenth place in the order of nations (in absolute terms) and being overtaken by all the countries of the G8 and also by Spain, Sweden and the Netherlands.

Civil societies retain their mature sensitivities. One such sensitivity may be to a Christian environment, for example. This is not to be undervalued; on the contrary, it is a source of relief. From the end of the 1960s, a renewed vision in the Catholic Church has made the relationship between north and south into the "new social issue" which had taken the place of the proletariat as the social problem within capitalist society.

The Catholic Church remains, perhaps, the most important institution binding Africa to the rest of the world, not only through its humanitarian interventions, but by joining African Catholics to a vast international network. Sections of the European Left have also made Africa the benchmark for international politics and morality.

Other forms of presence are rising over the African horizon and are different from the European ones. China has totally abandoned the military stance which led it to support revolutionary movements and states. Afro-Chinese commercial exchanges have tripled in five years, because of Chinese hunger for petroleum (30% of Chinese crude is African) and for timber and minerals. There are 700 Chinese companies operating today in 49 African states, regardless of the type of regime. The growth in Sino-African trading is stunning: from 2002 to 2003 it went up by 50%, and in the course of the next year by 60%. Since 2003, China has overtaken the United States and Great Britain as suppliers of goods to Central and West Africa. It is too soon to speak of a new cold war in the dark continent, but there is fierce competition. The United States are attentive to Africa from an economic point of view. Paul Wolfowitz, the president of the World Bank (the organization which works for African development) is drawing the attention of Washington to the continent. Africa is not a field reserved for the European world, and is becoming less so all the time. But, for the first time, Europe has become defeatist and has not adjusted its vision of the continent. Its policies waver between moral impulses and realism, between flare-ups of interest and lack of interest.

Nevertheless the stability of Africa is a necessary condition for European security. I realise that people who only think of the future within the confines of Europe, will take this assertion as a mask for kind-heartedness. Not so: it is an expression of enlightened self-interest. Today no continent can think of itself in isolation. Even American security must take account of the Middle East. Europe cannot think of itself in isolation when, by its very nature, it is a porous reality with multiple connections. Europe will have no peace if Africa has no peace. We must have the courage to take a long-term view which is able to make the most of our common history and our many, many connecting networks. For Europe, Africa is worth more than its 1.8% of world trade and 1% of world investment. On Africa Day 2001 Carlo Azeglio Ciampi, the President of the Italian Republic, declared, "We have an epoch-making task before us: to link the future of Africa to that of Europe, both steadily and firmly." Italian politics has not taken in that message. In Great Britain, a country which has re-positioned itself vis-à-vis Africa, Prime Minister Blair chose to have a Ministry for Development and identified Africa as a principal theme for the G8 in July 2005, following the fatal attacks in London. Linking Africa to Europe shows, at one and the same time, morality in politics and a realistic perspective on the world.

After the war, in 1948, a great French thinker, Emmanuel Mounier, wrote to the youth of Africa, "Eurafrican civilization, of which you are the pioneers, has yet to find its structures… Can we really speak of a Eurafrican world? Eurafrica can be a framework within which both the Europeans and the Africans look to their future. Geopolitics had already spoken of Eurafrica. In 1934, Paolo d'Agostino di Camerota wrote about it from a perspective of Fascist expansionism. He brought this perspective up to date in 1957 at the Treaties Committee in Rome saying that, as far as he was concerned, there was a Eurafrican community because it comprised several African regions. Back in the 1950s, Anton Zischka, in a book entitled *Africa*, envisaged Africa as "the first task for a unitary Europe". Moreover, as the European Community started, it had the problem of Africa put clearly before it. With his concept of a Franco-African community, de Gaulle launched a French Eurafrica, and welcomed African representatives into French institutions. But that construct collapsed under the weight of the spirit of independence and because of sparse French willingness to share government with Africans. When we speak of Eurafrica today we are not digging up ancient structures but pointing to an area in which European and African countries might be linked together in one system. In years gone by the Africans were evidently not free enough to manage it; today they are.

When I speak of Eurafrica I am not alluding to a political structure but to a vision and a system embracing the diverse European and African national identities. Eurafrica should be a policy and also a linking together of sentiments and ideas between worlds which have discovered that they are neighbours. President Senghor of Senegal launched the idea of Eurafrica in the same year as Mounier. Senghor – a poet and scholar as well as a politician and inventor of negritude – is an archetypal expression of the cross-breeding of Franco-European and African culture. His tone in speaking of Eurafrica was lyrical, "The two continents are complementary, because they are opposites like man and woman... For him Eurafrica was expressed primarily in culture. African writers do express a clear cultural crossbreeding, with their use of European languages. Between 1988 and 1996, 1,500 new titles of African literature were published.

At a time when economics counts for everything and people in Africa are dying of hunger, this way of speaking could appear poetic. Yet it evokes a feeling of communality which people need. Europeans need it as they ask about the meaning and function of their own countries. Eurafrica offers us a worthwhile perspective on how we can react reciprocally to the interest with which the Africans are looking to Europe. It offers a perspective through which to consider emigration and co-operation. It deals not only with making political choices but also with how to develop a feeling and a Eurafrican vision. Africa must commend itself more strongly as a European concern and interest, not in any imperialistic way (not that it would have either the strength or the desire for that) but from the standpoint of politics and society. To achieve this, it seems necessary to develop contacts at a social level, facilitating transfers of resources and support.

A Europe without the hegemony of one nation and Africa without the hegemony of one power are converging realities. The demographic future of Europe can draw support from Africa, because the old continent (precisely because it is ageing) is having to take into account that the size of its population will determine its future. Can Africa be for Europe as Latin America is for North America? History never repeats itself, nor would we want a new hegemony, but the future can lie in the developing of a system of solidarity and reciprocity. This can look like a marriage of unequals. The average Italian income is around 20,000 dollars a year; in Sub-Saharan Africa it is about 500 dollars, whilst the world average is 4,900 dollars. But Africa has its own strength, it own resources, the youth of its people and countries that are making progress... Above all, Africa is independent. No one can or should discuss independence any more and everyone is convinced that the Africans must work out their future themselves. But they must go forward together.

Eurafrica shows us the sadness of divisions in human society. Perhaps this is the whispered message which our countries need for their thinking through of world politics. Fellow feeling and culture must be involved, because no partnership between Africans and Europeans is possible without them. Eurafrica is significant for Africa. It opens up a vision of collaboration and cultural communality; it offers anchorage points for international relations and holds out the prospect of good neighbourliness. It is more meaningful for

103

Europe than simply economic interests. Europe can never be a greater Switzerland, protecting its own welfare and accepting only a few immigrants. Europe is not an empire. It is not even a former empire, such as Russia. It will be neither the United States nor China. Europe is something new, it is a Union noted in other areas of the world for the originality of this concept. But Europe without a "mission" will end up collapsing into itself. Eurafrica is not yet a political reality but from this time onwards it is a prospect for the future. This is the historic tapestry, complete with its ideals and political life, which our countries need. By having this perspective they will avoid the impossible pursuit of "purity" from contamination by the world's problems. They will also save themselves from wearing themselves out in a life that lacks perspectives on the world.

CHAPTER 5

ISLAM: FANTASY AND REALITY

Confronting an enemy or understanding a reality?

Today Islam seems to be the principal obstacle to people living together. Has Islam not always been the historic adversary of the West? Even the most liberal groups are embarrassed by the disconcerting aspects of world Islam. Whatever we may think, the brutality of the attacks by Al Qaeda and other terrorist groups brings us pointed reminders of the problem named Islam. This is no new situation, even though it has not been felt for a long time. Yet, during little more than twenty-five years, Islam has emerged as the great unknown of the future. We have to take account of it, but we do not know how. We certainly cannot use political and economic means, as happens with China. We are not dealing with any ordinary religion because Islam – as we hear from all sides – is at one and the same time a religion, a political stance and a culture.

In the space of a quarter of a century, Islam has passed from being something that was generally of little interest or of interest only as folklore, to attracting the anxious attention of many people – more expert or less so – who talk a very great deal about it. The social sciences used to apply the "more modernity less religion" dogma of secularization to the Muslim world, as it did to all religions. Given the march of progress, what happened in Western Europe ought to have happened in the Muslim world as well: namely, the decay of religion in public and private affairs.

In 1979, the revolution led by Khomeini forced the power of Islam into general awareness. Some sections of the political Left were briefly fascinated by such a popular rising, until they took note of its inner nature. As an ally of Shah Reza Pahlevi (a modernizer of Iran), the United States was straightaway opposed to the Khomeini regime. There seemed a pronounced imbalance of forces. Something similar had occurred at the end of the nineteenth century between the British and the revolt of the Mahdi, who was preaching a return to pure Islam and the rejection of whatever was unfaithful and 'Turkish' (which meant Egyptian and corrupt). The Mahdi's cherished dream was to breathe new life into the Muslim world, but his revolt suffered bloody suppression.

The story of Iran under the Ayatollahs is different. The network through which it spreads its message, the power of its state and the support of the masses make it an attractive powerhouse whose example has affected Muslims well beyond the Shiites.

The problems of Islam were once the preserve of scholars; today they are perceived to be of vital importance and occupy the front pages of newspapers. When I think about Islam, like everyone else I feel a sense of impotence. The question is too vast, it involves more than a billion people, and it covers widely differing political situations; giants like Pakistan and Indonesia and the whole Arab world. What is Islam? Where is it? Who are the Muslims?

One cannot even manage to express the problem of Islam in indistinct, generalized terms; one is simply struck dumb by it. Or else one goes to the Qur'an and other sources and finds confirmation of the nature of a violent or, instead, a peaceable religion. In the foundation documents of religions there is a mysterious complexity which defies simplifications and the passage of the centuries. Next comes the problem of exegesis and how these texts apply to the present day. But the Islam of

106

the present time cannot be explained from the foundation texts of Islam. Fareed Zakaria, an American political analyst of Indian origin, has stated, "There is little to be gained by searching in the Qur'an for the foundations of the true nature of Islam." One must keep in mind that Islamic history from its beginnings has had a close relationship with political power: this is written on to its chromosomes. In contrast, new-born Christianity lived through its earliest period as a minority and persecuted religion. However, even this has not prevented there being times of exclusivist Christianization of power and society.

Islam is huge, varied, contradictory and stratified, covering differing nations, cultures, languages, civilizations and economies. To see Islam as a global problem is a simplification produced by our culture and by our ignorance. But there is also the success of radicalism, whose high point is represented by bin Laden. In *Jihad: Rise and Fall*, a book published pre-9/11, Gilles Kepel states that, thanks to media coverage, this Saudi man's spectacular terrorism has made him into the agent of the *ummah*, the entire Muslim community. The attack on New York was the moment of the "consecration" of our image of global Islam. Al Qaeda has succeeded in turning itself into a network, with various cells in many parts of the world looking to it as their head. Even though they are not united organically, they are on the same wavelength as the messages that come from the Sheikh of Terror. The clever media strategy behind many of Al Qaeda's messages aims to create a position of leadership for itself across the total Muslim community, having no territorial base but having disciples scattered throughout the world. The leadership desires to represent the *ummah*. It is opposed to the West and is struggling against the other Muslim leaders, beginning with the Saudis. Islamic radicalism has as its chief aim the beating down of "impious" Muslim rulers: its expectation is for a struggle within Islam prior to being anti-West. Because of its successes, this armed struggle is legitimizing the radicals or the terrorists in the minds of the Muslim masses.

If Islamic terrorism is the true face of more than a billion believers, or if it is the definitive revelation about their religion, then the situation is indeed very grave. There may be no way out of it. There has been no shortage of alarm-bells ringing, and people like Oriana Fallaci, have had great success in drawing the media's attention to the situation. They have pointed to the dangers and suggested that there is a contrasting Western identity to Islam. Islam is a deadly threat, so what policies flow from that? Correcting his first statement after 11 September, Bush has consistently declared that America is not in a war against Islam but against terrorism and barbarity. Nevertheless the expectation of an imminent clash between civilizations (or with the West) still remains.

In a book whose title describes its line of argument, *The Islamic Christian Civilization*, Richard Bulliet has attempted to reconstruct a shared community of interests between their two worlds. He makes an analysis of a factor now in sharp crisis among Muslims: the traditional religious authority of the *ulema*. They fell into increasing discredit during the last two centuries under pressure from attempts at modernization which reinforced the imposition of innovation in an autocratic manner. The resistance of the *ulema* has been explained by those who fight against them as a phenomenon of traditionalism and therefore similar to European clericalism which vied with modernizing anticlericalism. In fact, the interpretation of Sharia Law by the *ulema* in Islamic history was as a limitation to the tyranny of monarchies which had to submit to it. Into the void left after monarchy and through the discrediting of religious authority, new demands have emerged, calling for the restoration of the Law; this began with the Muslim Brotherhood movement in the 1920s. Bernard Lewis says that

108

their dynamics are very different from those of Europeans who conceive of good government in terms of liberty, and not in terms of justice which is the case in Islam. Osama bin Laden aspires to present a religious leadership of a unitary, global Islamic world, the very opposite of those religious authorities which enjoy little credence. He argues this by reference to the suppression of the Caliphate in 1924.

To understand questions about Islam as if it were a single "subject" (based on a single, anti-West strategy) is to accept the representation of the world constructed by the Sheikh of Terror and by hard-line radicals. However, we cannot honestly accept that image of opposition between Christianity and Islam as an ancient idea and apparently a constant fact of history. I recall, a little after 9/11, a secularist Italian editor talking to me about the situation and saying that he felt himself to be a Christian – 9/11 had even signalled a rediscovery of Christian identity. He was very insistent on Christianity as a valuable mark of identity. However, I do believe that what drives such people is the anxiety that is caused by the present sense of emptiness, and therefore they are searching for further dimensions to life. This is not only a political commentary on Christianity and the West, it is just as much about faith in general.

To belittle the debate about the conflict of civilizations could seem a sort of surrender or tribute to political correctness. If terrorism does not bow us down, the Muslim demographic bomb certainly will. A novel has recently been published in Russia called *The Mosque of Notre Dame de Paris*. The author, Elena Cudinova, tells a story of Paris in 2047, dominated by Islam with the Christians ghetto-ized. Russian public opinion is very sensitive to the risk of a self-assertive Muslim population. But, in an important book, *The Third Church*, Philip Jenkins, an American historian of religions, shows that he is convinced that Islam will not overcome Christianity. The world is not one big Lebanon, where the Muslim population is inevitably eroding the position of Christians.

According to Jenkins, the Christian world will be more or less equivalent to the Islamic from a population point of view. Important countries will remain Christian (United States, Russia, Brazil, Mexico); others will have large Christian populations, even if there are conspicuous Islamic minorities (Philippines, Congo, Uganda, Germany); others will be balanced between Muslims and Christians, (Nigeria, Ethiopia and Tanzania). Pakistan, Bangladesh, Turkey, Iran and some others will be Muslim, whilst Indonesia, Egypt and Sudan will accommodate Christian minorities. Jenkins concludes, "Of the twenty-five largest nations in the world at the mid-point of the twenty-first century, twenty will be predominantly, if not entirely, Christian or Muslim. On the hypothesis that the present balance of religions is maintained until then, there will be a striking parity between Muslim and Christian strengths." Nine large countries will be Muslim, eight Christian and three divided.

The Islamic demographic bomb is a relative factor. Olivier Roy notes that no Muslim demography as such actually exists. In the year 2000, Indonesia, the most populous Islamic country, reckoned on 2.6 children per woman, whilst in the Catholic Philippines 3.6 children were arriving per woman. Future Christianity – and this is relevant – will belong more to the South of the world. Jenkins uses "Third Church" to denote this. This Christianity will be strongly charismatic and neo-Protestant and less identified with the historic Churches. This is no small question, but it does not apply to Islam.

Pluralist Islam or global Islam

Every attack and clash brings out again the confrontation between Christianity / the West and Islam, as if it were something archetypal, some deep-rooted destiny of history. Nevertheless, over the last two centuries (and maybe before then, since the defeat of the Ottomans before the gates of Vienna at the end of the seventeenth century), this confrontation has vanished. European countries have occupied the Muslim world. The practice of Islam has become a wall behind which Muslims have tried to preserve their identity, as was the case of the ulema movement in French Algeria, aiming to defend their religion and the Arab language against assimilation. Yet, there has not only been conflict between Christians and Muslims. Some years ago, in *Mediterranean: Cohabitation and Conflict between Christianity and Islam*, I tried to illustrate some situations where Jews, Muslims and Christians live together, even if it is not on equal terms. In the course of its victorious advance – and in the centuries which followed – Islam eroded away Christianity on the southern shore of the Mediterranean, but, whilst affirming its own superiority as the definitive revelation, it allowed Christianity and Judaism to survive since they are religions of the Book.

It is true that these cohabitations have been in deep crisis for some decades. The exodus of a million Jews from the Arab world means that almost all of them have gone since the end of the Second World War and the foundation of Israel. Christians in Turkey almost disappeared during the First World War and the Greco-Turkish crisis. Christian Arabs are emigrating. There are non-Arab Christian minorities in Islam: about 2% in Pakistan and 10% in Indonesia. The slimming down of the Christian minorities in the Arab world is a serious matter for those countries. Even though they may have held them in low esteem, they found them a positive expression of difference and pluralism. In the Middle East, the presence of Christian Arabs (from whom came some important people for the cause of Arab nationalism) has again brought into question the total identification of Arab-ness and Islam. The presence

111

of minorities can play an important part in the choices and self-presentation of majorities.

However, those Christian minorities do not worry much about Western politics. We have seen this in the clashes suffered by Christians in Sudan. We are seeing it in Iraq, where the new constitution recognises Sharia Law as its guiding source and reduces the secular character of the state, leaving the Christian minority – which was in the country before the Islamic conquest – in an insecure position. As the Chaldean Patriarch of Iraq, Bidawid, and authoritative Syrian bishops have told me, the majority of Christians always considered the secular regime of the Baath party in both Iraq and Syria to be a guarantee against radical Islam. John Paul II was concerned at the impact of the Gulf wars on the situation of Christians in the Middle East and their cultural links. The secular policy of Christian forces going to the defence of Oriental Christians created many problems for those minorities. We talk a great deal about Muslim minorities in Europe but very little about those Christians who live in the Muslim world. It would perhaps be interesting to question ourselves about this matter.

We must look at the Muslim world in a coherent way. Who represents it? There are no "Popes" in Islam (except, partly, among the Shiites); the political leaders (pro-West) do not represent the Muslim masses. As we have said, the fantasy of a confrontation between two worlds keeps raising its head, as we ask ourselves whether the majority of Muslims might be radical, therefore their governments illegal. Does Al Qaeda represent a global Islam which now has ascendancy over the Muslim masses? Olivier Roy wrote, "The new factor introduced by Islam's move into the West is the disconnection of Islam from an explicit culture." This is an important observation: globalized Islam is not connected to the culture and traditions of Muslim countries, things which deeply influence the way of life and faith. Global Islam is to be found in areas of Muslim immigration.

It is noteworthy that the young attackers in London in July 2005 were children of well-integrated Pakistani families. In radicalism lying outside their formal education, these young people had found a way of breaking with their families, over and beyond their hatred of the West, where they had been born, grown up, and whose children they were. However, in Holland a reconsideration of the murder of Theo van Gogh brings us into contact with a world of social marginalization, in which the Dutch libertarian-individualistic model of society has scored notable failures. The Islam to which those young people are 'returning' is not that of their countries, linked to history and tradition. Rather, it is the Islam of preachers who have come from the Middle East, especially the *wahabiti*: this is "pure" Islam, lacking any history. In this sense they are not returning but are converting to something new. Their conversion is often the fruit of frustration but also comes from a desire to show off their difference in a society where they feel they are irrelevant. This is an Islamic choice but it has a European flavour. The communities of their choice are not those of the emigrant communities of their own country. Their Islam is "pure" and global. It is similar to that of the veterans of Islamic internationalism (the Islamic belt against the Soviets) or the virtual *ummah* of the Internet.

But global Islam does not represent the very developed complexity that is the Muslim world. Partly, but not only, because of the power of the media, every element of the Muslim world is having to reposition itself as it comes face to face with the globalization of Islam. For Muslims the 1990s were a period of restructuring its identity between fundamentalist insurgency and Westernized globalization. The Muslim world is passing through a period of grave turbulence. There are so many and such differing cultural and religious situations to cope with. Global, radicalized Islam has its strategy of attack. The primary objective is the ruling powers of the Islamic

113

countries: Saudi, Egypt (remember the spectacular attack in which President Sadat met his death), the petroleum-producing monarchies, Tunisia, Syria and so on. In spectacular style, terrorism is demonstrating its ability to guide the Muslim world into confrontation with the West. This confrontation has been worked up over more than a century by putting this question, "Why are we Muslims backward compared with the West?" The fundamentalist answer is a return to Islam (but to what sort of Islam?); it is radicalizing itself and, in some of its sections, becoming terrorism. Beginning from the Muslim Brotherhood of Hasan al Banna or from the Pakistani Abul Ala Mawdudi, radicalism has orientated itself more and more into thinking of Islam as a political ideology which will contribute to the rebirth of Islamic society.

These ideas find themselves in a confused Muslim world, loaded with frustrations against the West and Israel. The greatness of Islam in the past is often referred to by way of comparison. Bernard Lewis makes this observation on the disappointing results for the reformers and the revolutionaries who are, "seeking well-being through creating economic development in some countries which have impoverished and corrupt economies... But their worst results have been in the field of politics." Socialism and nationalism failed in the time of "thirdworldism". Since 1989, from Eastern Europe to the countries of Africa, to South Africa and Asia, the world has been opening up to democratic systems (despite their many imperfections and stresses), but the Arab world has remained almost entirely in the hands of dictators. From an economic standpoint, the comparison with Asian development is a further humiliation.

The rift with the West has grown wider. Arab nationalism, embodied by Nasser, had identified a scapegoat and an enemy in the shape of Western imperialism. Until the 1950s the United States was popular in Egypt, unlike France and Great Britain

114

who were held to be imperialist countries (one thinks of the Suez crisis of 1956). Then anti-Americanism grew up. It had its birth in Nazi propaganda and the German culture of the 1930s, which had become spread throughout the Arab world. It was reinforced by the cold war, Marxist and Soviet propaganda, "thirdworldism", and, lastly, by the world hegemony of the United States. Sayyid Qutb, a Muslim Brotherhood theorist condemned to death by Nasser in 1966, spent a long time in the United States, during which he developed a very critical view of the materialism and religiosity of the Americans, despite the large number of churches there. Lewis sums up, "The immorality and dissipation of America and the consequent threat which it posed to Islam and to Muslim nations became an article of faith in fundamentalist circles."

There is a form of anti-Semitism that is not traditional in Islam. Yet anti-Semitism has become a source of nourishment in the campaign against Israel, and it also feeds a conspiracy view of the world. *Protocols of the Elders of Zion* was translated by Christian Arabs and began to circulate in the Islamic world. The struggle with Israel has done the rest. It is only in the last few years that at international talks there has been some success in bringing together some, but not all, religious Muslims with religious Jews. Anti-Westernism, anti-Semitism, the idea of there being a conspiracy against Islam, political frustration and economic failure have all combined to form a magma which explains the difficulties of the Muslim world and then finishes up by attributing the responsibility for the difficulties to the West. The abyss opened up between Western politics and anti-Western nationalism has grown larger.

During the period from the 1970s to the 1990s, Arab nationalism crumbled away, but Khomeini was affirmed in Iran. Fundamentalist ideals are the recipe for "Islam's 1968" (forgive the juxtaposition) and are capable of motivating

115

revolution against political forces. These ideals were also spread by Saudi propaganda supported by the petrodollar, especially in the period of the petroleum crises. The wisdom of the religious policies of the Saudi *dawa* remains a matter for consideration; I refer to their mission which has spread *wahabita* radicalism into many corners of Islam. Young men raised in this school, cut off from the traditional culture of their fathers, have disputed with the Islamic leaders of their countries and even with the Saudi authorities themselves. What have been the consequences of this Saudi religious investment among Palestinians, in Africa, in Pakistan, and in so many parts of the *ummah*? Yet, for over sixty years, Saudi Arabia has at the same time been an ally of the United States.

This complex mix of ideas and radical sentiments has changed aspects of Marxist and "thirdworldist" language and militancy. One symbolic event was the conversion to Islam of the international terrorist Carlos in the time when Sudan was ruled by Hassan Tourabi (who later surrendered him to France). In Lebanon, Imam Moussa Sadr – who disappeared in mysterious circumstances in 1978 – politicized the Shiite minority, motivating it to be an armed movement demanding social change. Among Shiites, Ali' Shariati, an Iranian intellectual, played an important part: he had been a student in Paris, had had contact with Marxism and Islamology, and died in 1977 before the Khomeini victory. Shariati introduced revolutionary streams of thought into Islamic politics, creating a synthesis of Marxist thinking and Islamic vision. He translated Fanon's *The Wretched of the Earth*, the Bible of the Third World. He was also opposed to Shiite clericalism and worked out a theology of Islamic liberation. So the Iranians, also using their knowledge of diffused political thought and western philosophy (which was superior to that of the Sunni world), created a synthesis of Islam and Marxism through revolutionary thought and religious radicalism. For Khomeini, the world divides into the

116

oppressors and the oppressed. His position concerning the cold war was: "Neither East nor West, only Islam".

Radical currents have run through Islam. Their content and their militant language have taken over the hearts and minds of the youth culture. The radicalised world is made up of young, urbanized people and those with few prospects for the future. It finds no anchorage in nationalism, like the preceding generation, but finds it in the simplicity of the Islamic formulae which seem to be eternal, "Islam is the answer to everything". On the threshold of the 1990s, the Arab, Iranian and Islamic world in general was a society notable for an increase in its youth population. It is also noteworthy that France before its revolution, the United States before '68, and Iran before its revolution all went through a time of powerful population increase. It is in this sense that we can speak of "Islam's 1968" as a movement, transnational in character, marked by diversity and concurrency. This movement has channelled frustrations and hopes and has offered a language for thinking through the alternative to the political and social status quo. It retains the eternal flavour of its religion but it also has the modern flavour of utopianism and uses modern means, primarily videocassettes, Internet and technologies of every kind and sort to do its work.

Facing up to these radical currents has today become a serious problem. The struggle against terrorism is grave and urgent. Not all fundamentalists are terrorists, even if we do find among them those who support suicide actions in Israel (like Daradawi, the Al Jazeera preacher who is also against attacks on the West). Not all fundamentalists are represented by terrorist actions, although Islamic territory is the place where this type of activity is cultivated. If we must not see naïve similarities, it is still necessary to recognize real connections. There are not two Islams: one radical and one moderate, which is how we often talk in the West. This defining of moderate Islam (excluding

117

liberal Muslims, an important but minority constituency) has little to do with its reality and it is basically weaker on the more "religious" demands of radicalism.

There are so many Islams and so many Muslim countries with differing histories and settings. It is not enough to make spectacular terrorism the image of all Islam. There is a force within parts of the real Islam that resists radicalism. This force caused Gilles Keppel to say in 2000 that fundamentalism is in crisis. After 9/11, the same author focused the predicament of Islam around the idea of *fitna*, disorder and anarchy which runs across the world which feels threatened by external aggression. There is a widespread fear that Muslim "land" will be trampled by infidels. For decades the Palestine question has been a recurring theme with which Muslims identify. Also, think of Bosnia, of Kashmir which is claimed by the Pakistanis, think of Chechnya (where an ancient Muslim struggle against Russia has been restarted)... then think of the part played by the war in Iraq and the presence of Western troops in that country. Terrorism has fitted itself powerfully into this picture as a struggle against Westerners and Islamic traitors. Yet today Iraq is showing itself to be a country where links between Islamists and nationalists can operate.

"Islam feels it is under attack and is responding by fighting in a united way": that is a naïve simplification easy to state in the media, but it is false. Islam is not one unit: there are many Islams, as many as there are Islamic countries. There is the force of realism, of different national interests and cultures. Terrorism can get Muslim governments into serious difficulty but it cannot enfold them all into its own attitudes. Above all, it is essential to draw a distinction (maybe not always clear even in my own explanations) between the Islam of the "great Middle East" (including North Africa and Iran) and the remainder of the Muslim world. Fareed Zakaria maintains, "The true problem is not in the Muslim world but in the

Middle East," adding, "Not one of the twenty-two countries who are members of the Arab League is an electoral democracy, whereas, if one considers states throughout the world, sixty-three per cent are." Zakaria is right to speak of "political failure" and deeply rooted cultures of authoritarianism. Yet conditions are different in the case of Indonesia (recently democratised), or Pakistan (whose primary reason for existing is Islam) and for the 140 million Muslims of India.

It is important to explain the pluralistic reality of Islam, even to the Muslims themselves. The role of information, television (think of the success of *Al Jazeera* and its international impact) or the Internet are making a positive contribution in the Arab world. Renzo Guolo has observed, "The perception that one can express one's own opinion without falling under the axe of some ever-threatening power, the possibility of considering opinions different from the official line has passed the point of no return." Inside the Muslim world a more articulate public opinion is growing up, even if it seems to be only slightly liberal and too close to the fundamentalists and to the internal language of Islam.

Islamic fundamentalism would like to standardize the Arab world (and the rest of Islam) on the model used by nationalisms. These very often work within the borders of a particular national area. Pan-Arab nationalism has failed. Will radical Islam be able to construct a single Muslim nation? Plurality does exist and it is strong. It needs freedom to express itself. Instead there is political and cultural poverty. In Egypt (the cultural heart of the Arab world) 375 books are published each year compared with 4,000 in Israel. The great Tunisian intellectual Mohammed Talbi (Islamic scholar but still a man of European culture) has shrewdly written that the impoverishment of the Arabs and their backwardness compared with Israel depends on their lack of liberty. Because of this, some throw themselves into violence,

119

"When pens are broken, all that remains is knives. Few choices are left: silence, prison or crime. In every case the victim is thought."

It is not enough to spread democratic methods, what also need to be developed are liberty, debate, the appreciation and respect of differences and education in how to control conflicts by political rather than violent means. The whole Arab world has paid a price for the depression of Lebanon (through its civil war and Syrian occupation) because Lebanon had been a space for shedding the sweetness and light of pluralist sentiment and cultural debate. The Christian minorities are an influence for liberty in the Muslim world. Ethnic minorities in the Arab world are an important reality: we can see this with the secular Kurds in Iraq or the Kabili in Algeria and Morocco. The emergence of pluralism in the Arab and Muslim world is the defeat of terrorist, totalitarian Jihadism. John Paul II's intuition about the Communist world applies also to the Islamic world, although they are so different: reinforce the reality of what nations have within them and emphasize liberty and pluralism as well.

Islam and democracy

We must now ask the age-old question of whether Islam is compatible with democracy. The question is posed frequently and people tend to address it in a somewhat "fundamentalist" way, concentrating on the origins of Islam. Huntington seems to believe in incompatibility. But democracy is not a philosophical problem; it is a way of proceeding. Democracy has a practical history. The organic nature of Islam is not an insuperable barrier, despite its scant distinction between the individual and the community and its lower respect for pluralism. Many scholars are trusting to the impact of European democracy on

Islam. The effect of dictatorships has been very negative: widespread authoritarianism (the hallmark of its mentality) has caused opposition, stirred up by fundamentalists. The myth put about by the progressives of there being opposition from society has backfired, extolling radical Islam which is very active in creating social networks, in contrast to the present state of affairs. Leaving dictatorships or semi-dictatorships in the field ends up by making fundamentalist opposition grow. They undoubtedly have an insecure future, and what are the alternatives to risking an attempt at democracy?

In Turkey, fundamentalism has been integrated into democratic life through the AKP led by Erdogan, the Party for Justice and Development, the successor to the Islamic Refah which was dissolved by the military in 1997. This integration has happened despite widespread distrust over possible abuses of the democratic processes. The strong power of the military is being a guarantee and a counterweight to fundamentalist government in secular Turkey. Also Kuwait, Morocco and Jordan, even despite the role of the monarch (and sometimes because of his religious functions), have allowed some funda-mentalist tendencies into political life.

In 1994-5, in Rome, the Community of Sant'Egidio hosted the launch of a "platform" for the transition to democracy in Algeria. This brought together secularists, nationalists and the Islamic Salvation Front. Sant'Egidio had noted the crises in Algeria and the developing terrorism and rebellion which had followed on from the interruption of its electoral processes in 1992. This had handed a trump card to the fundamentalists in the ISF. However, the government and the military authorities rejected the "platform"; some of them thought it was offering the hand of friendship to the enemies of freedom.

The idea had been to line up the fundamentalists alongside the other political forces and thus avoid a dramatic civil war. Military power could have been a counterweight. Besides that, in the Rome "platform" (which gathered together a swathe of political authorities), no one spoke of *sharia* as the source of law and they also solemnly renounced violence as an instrument for winning power or hanging on to it. Much of this was later taken up by President Bouteflika when he negotiated with the armed fundamentalists of the ISF. The cost of the Algerian war was 100,000 dead, plus the infliction of deep traumas on society. These must be resolved in the aftermath of the violent actions by the terrorists and a policy to build security must be followed.

Democracies are not only the affirmation of the will of the majority; they can also assume the role of protector of liberties. In South Africa, what allowed the painless transition from the apartheid regime were guarantees for the white minority, for the Zulus and for others: the majority does not have absolute power. Democracy is developed by means of such counterweights. The role of the military in Turkey is another example of this. In Albania, where Socialists and Democrats had reached a kind of "bipolarism" of hatred (with the winners in 1997 abusing their power over the losers), the Community of Sant'Egidio proposed a pre-electoral guarantee agreement which is still holding good to this day. The agreements controlling the peace-making in Burundi offer guarantees to the Tutsi minority concerning control of the Senate. The Lebanese scholar Ghassan Salame describes the need for counterweights in his proposal for "pre-electoral pacts between those in power and the various opposition groups, Islam included". He added, "It goes without saying that such pacts for the gradual adoption of representative democracy would only be possible if Islamists accept that their choices made when in power could be reversed and that their policies could be legitimately opposed." Pre-electoral pacts can become important guarantees which moderate the wishes of the majority in a democracy.

There is no alternative to democracy in opening up the road to freedom, even if anti-liberal minorities can also profit from it. This is an old problem for democracy. People may ask, "Would not freedom for the Communist Party in the period following the Second World War have been used to demolish democracy?" And "Would not liberty have been wiped out?" The power of the Communist Party was enormous throughout the country of Italy. Yet, despite pressures to the contrary, De Gasperi and Pius XII accepted democratic contest, although aware that there was no infallible security for the future.

So, if the fundamentalists triumph in our day, what kind of future will democracy have? This is what was at stake in Algeria when, in 1992, the electoral process was interrupted. I remember that one person of international standing – the then secretary of the UN, Boutros Boutros Ghali – lent his support to this decision. Today, the Hamas fundamentalists have won elections to the Palestinian authority. Israel and the international community are now faced with some serious choices. But, if Hamas wants to govern, will it not have to make changes that are realistic? In another instance, in Iran, a hardline Khomeinist candidate, Ahmedinejad has won recent Iranian elections. This may also have been partly due to a system of filtering candidacy which was imposed politically. Ahmedinejad is restarting the nuclear programme and wants to turn his country into a power with a similar status to India or China. One only hopes that experience in government will teach him a lesson in realism. If the opposite happens, the problems arising will be hard. In another region, the United States have created westernized outposts without popular democratic support and the results have been disastrous; consider Latin America.

Some people maintain it is impossible to make too many distinctions in the Muslim world, because what we are dealing with is a new form of Nazism. However, we are not in fact faced with a recently formed political movement but rather by political and religious streams flowing from an ancient religious world. The problem is not whether or not to have dealings with Islam but rather how to describe all the deep differences inside that world: differences between Arabs and non-Arabs, differences between those with mature experience of free debate and others used to religious and ethnic pronouncements, differences between those traits which are inherent in the whole fundamentalist world and those that are rooted in the current interests, as well as the histories of individual Muslim countries. Democratization cannot be guaranteed in absolute terms, but is a risk to be accepted. It grows out of many political, cultural and economic factors. The West can aid this development.

Geography and history are calling upon us to live with Muslims, before we live with Islam. Because of this, the confrontation between the West and Islam lies in the way the encounter (and eventually the clash) is to be expressed, and not in the global impact to which the logic of Al Qaeda seems to be pulling us, exploiting our over-simplifications. The "clash-between-two-worlds" scenario corresponds to ancient archetypal thinking that is easily transmitted by the modern media. Pronouncement-making is not only a way to peace; it is also a way to severe and actual confrontation. We are over-fond of simplifications, even when they make our blood run cold. So we must perhaps become used to complexity, especially that of the Muslim world.

This is not how bin Laden describes matters: he presents us with a universe where the good is characterised by *jihad*, and everyone else is a bunch of wicked tyrants. In one of his feverish messages to the West, the Saudi terrorist declared, "they want dialogue, we want death." What is impressive about Islamic terrorists is not only the evil that they commit, but the cult of death for themselves as well. Suicide martyrdom, a modern reformulation of the *shahid*, an Islamic martyr, appeared in 1972 in an attack on Tel Aviv airport by three Japanese belonging to the Red Brigade, a terrorist splinter-group allied to the Marxist Front for the Liberation of Palestine. Their example spread rapidly among the Hezbollah in Lebanon and then into the rest of the Middle East. In the war between Iraq and Iran, a *shahid* was an Iranian who sacrificed himself or herself in the struggle. From 1980 to 1988, 200,000 Iranians died, 45% of them being between 16 and 20 years in age. Suicide martyrdom, terrorism, preaching hatred… these are indeed Islam – but not the whole of Islam.

Talbi, who knows the real Islam very well, talks of a "spiritual amputation of the human being" through its secularization. It is "no longer an individual adhering to the faith, but of belonging to a global ethnic community". It is secularization that is homogenizing the Islamic world as if it were one nation. The world of Talbi is Islamic and has behind it a great tradition and also many, many Muslims who are alive today. The world of the Indonesian Abdurrahman Wahid is Muslim; he is the former leader of the Nahdlatul Ulama (with 35 million members), and was President of his country from 1999 to 2001. For him, the idea of the Islamic state is correct for the Middle East, whilst among Asian Muslims a thrust for jihad is arriving by starting its re-interpretation amid changing situations. The world of Abou Bakar Bashir is also Islamic. He was condemned by the Indonesian Courts of Justice in 2003, although he was a supporter of the Islamic state. The future of Indonesia (87% Muslims in a population of 210 millions) is no secondary, minor matter for Islam. The situation of Bangladesh in Asia appears to be very complicated, with an aggressive fundamentalist presence, revealed in August 2005 with the almost simultaneous detonation of 450 bombs. This fundamentalism is worming its way into some parties in the political system; nevertheless it is meeting opposition from important democratic groups. Anwar

Ibrahim, a Malaysian, emphasises the value of cohabitation between diverse cultures and nations. There are so many Islams. To live with them, to be next to them across frontiers and in daily life, is not always easy; it is hard work. Their intrusion into globalized consumerism is not something "sweet", because it brings with it a new diversity and sometimes threats as well.

Can terrorism win? I think not. Not only because of the strength of the United States and Europe, not only because of the strength of its own Islamic roots and not only because of the strength of other powers in the life of the world (such as China, which they fear), but it will also not win because of the complexities and contradictions within Islam. Terrorism can make us suffer but it cannot win. For our part, we must not give in to a simplistic vision of Muslim people. We must not give in to this terrorist simplification but face it intelligently, based upon real understanding. The "dialogue" with Islam is not an expression of goodwill, something inherited from post-conciliar Catholicism (which hopefully has a sense of sin about the Crusades). It is not an unprejudiced negotiation with all people, asking just to be left in peace in order to increase our own quality of life. Dialogue is the ability to look the other person's differences in the face, to try and develop more ways of relating to them, to weave a pattern of relationships, and to gain a grasp of the interests and attitudes of the other person. The remainder – by which I mean the future – means taking the historic risk and knowing at the same time that nothing is certain.

CHAPTER 6

CIVILIZED COHABITATION

A difficult world to understand

In this book I have surveyed just some aspects of the times through which we are living today. There are plenty of others. We all flounder a bit when faced with such a complicated world. What is more, we know a great deal about this world; almost everything (if we wish to) when we consider the huge heap of information available. There is too much news in the media for anyone to digest it all. Television shows us every kind of crisis in every kind of place. We get to know everything quickly. There is so much information that we cannot absorb it. Sometimes we are seized by a feeling of sheer impotence in the face of situations that are far away and barely under-standable. For instance, it was like that at the time of the Rwandan crisis between the Hutus and the Tutsis. We grasped that something terrible was happening but it was hard to get our minds around it. Above all, we simply lack all the mental tools needed for explaining such phenomena.

Yet we cannot give proper attention – and be informed – unless we have at least some framework of interpretation, maybe to enable discussion with someone close to us. We need to find some kind of answer as we face up to what is unfolding before us. We all live on the terraces of the stadium of the world, or, rather, we are on that virtual information terrace which brings distant matters into close-up. Disorientation lies in wait for people who, until a few years ago, had followed events with a clear idea that good and justice lay with one side and not with the other. Today's complexity disorientates and confuses us. It is not easy to discuss or speak about international issues but it is easier to discuss internal politics, especially when they concern prominent leaders. Nevertheless, we are aware that we are all connected, that crises do spread and that threats do reach us, even if they come from afar. All said and done, we need to talk about international affairs today even more than we did in the past. Everything – I repeat – everything is very complicated. And we are living through the "happy hour" of drastic simplifications which sell us simple solutions for a barely decipherable world.

One mistake typical of globalized information is to devise questions that are increasingly generalized, whilst simultaneously aspiring to globalized answers. Such answers are improbable, often untenable, the fruit of simplifications but, nevertheless, they are effective in the media. Yet a vision of the present day which is meant to be realistic and unemotional can never avoid considering the complexities of the contemporary scene. Totalitarian ideologies were all an escape from complexity. They seemed to be indicating a secure interpretation of the present and the "scientific" road to the future. Even post-1989, neo-liberalism stated the scientific conviction that the market would succeed where the great empires, ideologies and religions had failed and that it would unite human beings into one global community. At least today we are all more thoughtful about similar certainties.

There are no simple answers to the question of how it might be possible for people to live together either at the international level or within a restricted local environment. Unsatisfactory answers have a harsh flavour and come from people who give negative answers and maintain that living together is impossible. Such people should be asked, "So what are we to do?" for we cannot live in isolation in the contemporary world where simply everything is being transmitted and communicated. Or they ought to be asking

128

themselves how many and what sort of wars will need to be fought. If we face up to the complexity of the real situation, it could be that more solutions will emerge than are offered by drastically simplified generalized questions and answers.

No more satisfactory are those sweet answers that come from a serene cosmopolitanism that feeds off a confidence that, in the end, the values of progress and democracy will prevail. Our destiny is not to be cosmopolitan; the reality and the reactions of people differ from each other. There are no answers that can widen out to become universal recipes for the identity and the history of the whole world, homogenizing what we are and how we live. The globalized world is made up of differences which will persist. To live with others, we must understand who they are and not merely state who we are and then offer our own models for living to the others. And yet, in spite of cultural differences, some general needs and universal values are re-emerging on all sides: at least, that is my personal experience.

Patience supported by commitment and hope are helping in the exploration of the human predicament in all its complexity. To think about the real situation means having the patience to have a practical involvement with it. Above all, as Tommaso Padoa-Schioppa wrote, "Seek to understand what it means for everyone; dedicate more time and attention to the amazing facts that are happening before our eyes." However, people are in a hurry and put their trust in whatever simplified formulas are being shouted out. We need to develop more of a taste for knowledge about our own day and age. To think about reality implies learning to have discernment. Indeed, discernment is fundamental to avoid creating monsters and phantoms in the laboratory of our own thinking, confusing different symptoms and expressions under the same classification.

Knowledge of history is essential, because realities, nations and identities persist through time, even if the external appearances change. As Karl Meyer wrote, "History is not a

129

programme, but a story that can put us on our guard. It contains a whole heap of warnings for those who believe they are able to anticipate the future or that their country has some special mandate from providence or that alliances are a mere nuisance." History does not offer lessons in living or easy prophecies, but it does help in getting a grasp of our own or the other person's stature. There are some puzzling coincidences but, on a variety of subjects in history, there is permanence in respect of organization and perspectives that last through time. Knowing about geopolitical and historical culture at every level is becoming as necessary as knowing the English language when we are travelling; they are the alphabet of discerning and they can read the true realities.

Everybody "reads" the present time from their own point of view, but we are also called upon to make a reasonable effort to think of possible answers to the questions about how we can live together. To do this we need to look the other person in the face and understand them, rather than looking at ourselves and our own group. Instead of superficial solutions, we need a new way of thinking about the future, where the great questions now facing the human race and the great questions posed by anthropology can meet. This seems to me a task for European culture: to find the courage to develop a patient understanding which relies on resources and information accumulated over decades. London and Paris are no longer capitals of empires but they are lived in by people who come from all over the world. They are in touch with very diverse areas and possess a huge concentration of cultural resources. To sum up, they are the expression of that kind of European culture which is able to have a steady grasp of contemporary realities without pretensions to neo-colonialism or hegemony. This is possible not only for London and Paris, but for very many other European cities and for the whole of European society in general.

A culture of common interests

European politics must not become a comedy lacking perspective. Europeans need to think politically and we need European leaders of international stature. John Paul II, a religious leader in the twentieth century, was a European with an intellect that embraced the whole world. He demonstrated the courage of patiently understanding the real situation and having a full encounter with it. As a man of the Church, he had his vision for the world and he advocated his faith strongly. Indeed, it was that faith which brought him into confrontation with so many aspects of life in the world. John Paul II believed in the subjective reality of nations, even when they were not enjoying political freedom. He refused to think of Eastern Europe as an entity in itself, merely an expression of Communism. Despite Soviet aggression, he was looking for a human community to encourage. That life-journey of his became an instrument of encounter. For John Paul II it was a necessary transition to make.

We must include this figure of the Pope within our common history which belongs to all people, not just to believers (Christian and non-Christian). Through the biography of this great European, we are able to approach the history of our time. Being at the head of Catholicism which is an international body, John Paul II grasped the value of the meaning of identity. His strategy in Poland had been to sustain a humiliated group in society which was expressing itself through Solidarity. The peaceful transition of the East to democracy (excepting Romania) became a model for him. The same transition to democracy in Pinochet's Chile seemed a success in his eyes, as was the peaceful exit of the Philippines from the Marcos dictatorship through popular pressure. This Pope did indeed believe in the non-violent strength of ideas, whilst being very critical of the use of warfare, because he too had been bitterly marked by the experience of the Second World War.

In 1986, amid the climate of the cold war and facing a culture still largely dominated by the idea that religions are irrelevant, John Paul II convened the leaders of world religions at Assisi to say "Never again" to confrontation between each other. After 9/11, in 2002, he convened a second such meeting at Assisi as a riposte to terrorism and to clashes between civilizations and religions. Led by John Paul II at Assisi, the Christians did not renounce their specific faith, drowning it in a sort of United Nations of religions. But they did declare that they wish to live in peace with the other religions. It is a pact of respect and peace, anchored in the roots of our faith. There exists no single universal religion for all people, nor is there a universal essence of religions. The spirit of Assisi is to live religiously inspired lives together.

Pope John Paul II combined the value of religious and national identity with the interests of a community which goes beyond the borders of any single country. He spoke many times of the United Nations Organization in this sense. Yet his deepest intuition was probably for the unity of Europe from East to West and he said this in times when no one thought that the Berlin Wall could ever fall. For John Paul, a single "geography of the depths" (to use an expression of Giorgio La Pira) connected something that appeared superficially divided. Moreover, the study of long-term history, done with the detachment of an historical method completely centred on events, does demonstrate deep structures which embrace and tie together different realities. Also, dissensions sometimes conceal connections which are being developed deep-down. Fernand Braudel could speak of the Mediterranean as a unitary system even in respect of areas and times heavy with conflicts.

Is the United Nations an encumbrance or does it, in its own way, represent uniting processes within the flow of history? In short, does it express a world-system? This is sometimes talked about in a ritual way. But we cannot let this institution go adrift, even if there are many problems, including a lack of trust in its activities. Despite its current discredited state, the UN represents the idea of a possible world order. In point of fact, in the decade between 1990 and 2002 it has deployed four armed actions for peace and six preventive diplomatic operations, which is more than in the forty previous years of its history. The UN expresses the idea that global public assets do exist, although menaced by the earth growing hotter, by pollution or by atomic weapons. Particularly notable is the complicated process of the acceptance of the Kyoto protocols (especially the refusal of the United States which considers them detrimental to American interests). It is necessary to deepen the awareness of these global public assets. Hurricane "Katrina", which struck Louisiana with an exceptionally destructive force, not only forces us to reflect on our relationship with our environment but also on the difficulties of states – even one like the USA – to deal with environmental crises by itself. Those who have lived through a number of decades do perceive that the climatic and environmental situation is changing and that new problems are arising. But individual states cannot cope alone, nor are they able to represent global public interest. Back in 1996, Nino Andreatta stated, "So as to preserve this fundamental public asset (the environment) to which the very survival of future generations is bound, it is necessary for the UN to draw up criteria for an equitable sharing of costs and benefits in the maintenance of resources."

Atomic weaponry also represents a threat to global public assets. Through the Chernobyl disaster, Europe experienced how the frontiers of states are no protection from such a threat. Besides, nuclear technology had been used in the business of the cold war as a powerful balancing factor – which was certainly a risk. The nuclear non-proliferation regime of the

133

1970s, integrated into the treaties in the 1990s, limited the development of nuclear weapons. After 1989, a world without nuclear weapons was the dream. But the situation has deteriorated because new states have come – sometimes covertly – into the atomic club. Today we speak less of the atomic threat than during the cold war. Nevertheless new atomic weapons are being developed, not so much for the sake of deterrence as for battlefield use. These are a "fourth generation", says Angelo Baracca; they get round the non-proliferation treaties and they constitute a real threat: "a phase of completely new nuclear proliferation has opened up..."

Sixty years on from Hiroshima (the nuclear explosion that caused 140,000 immediate deaths and 77,000 later ones), in addition to the five traditional nuclear powers – the USA with 6,390 bombs, Russia with 3,242, plus China, France and Great Britain with an arsenal from 100 up to 200 bombs, there are forty countries, such as Egypt and South Korea, which can manufacture atomic weapons. The history of experiments with these weapons is a tale of death. Out of the Soviet military personnel employed in these operations about 30,000 have died (only about one hundred are still alive). North Korea probably already possesses nuclear weapons. Israel has 200 bombs, India 150, and Pakistan 175. Further, many have access to so-called "dirty" atomic energy. The atomic menace has greatly increased since 1968, when 180 countries signed the Non-Proliferation Treaty. In a history during which millions of men and women have acquired greater awareness of themselves and control of their own destinies, just a few decision-makers are now able to initiate murderous conflicts.

So large a diffusion of atomic weapons demonstrates how we must manage to co-exist with countries which can destroy each other reciprocally. Fundamentally and in spite of its military (and atomic) power, Israel under Sharon took the decision to withdraw the Jewish settlements from Gaza because they had come to understand they had no alternative as they searched for a way of living with the Palestinians. Throughout the world the risk of terrorism persists, or of terrorist political groups gaining power. Atomic power obliges us to seek a responsible form of multi-polarity and presses for understanding between countries which have the ability to destroy each other. In this sense, an authority such as that of the UN needs to be rediscovered both by the various states and by public opinion in the nations.

A revolution in thought and way of Life

A culture needs to grow up in which national groups open their minds towards a bigger picture. Without a shared culture we cannot achieve much in our world and are risking a great deal if we try. Naturally there are many cultures, but when I speak of a "shared culture", I mean the awareness of needing to live together in a responsible way and having common convictions which go beyond our differences. These are not the convictions the ruling classes have inherited. So, to construct a shared culture, we must begin with the men and women of our own time. We find ourselves facing an extraordinary phenomenon which we need to note strongly: never in history have women and men been so literate as they are today and, therefore, they are communicators and potential users of new ideas and new cultures. Today, nothing will happen without them and without their involvement. This is no banal truism but an observation which becomes clear from many crisis situations.

We need to know how to talk with the men and women of our time, to motivate them and involve them. Although they are faced with great economic, political and atomic powers, people count for more than they did in times past. Because of this, authoritarian regimes without democratic participation are finding life ever more difficult. Even those undemocratic regimes have to take public opinion into account. Each authoritarian power needs increasingly to have the guarantee of a consensus of support, either by populism or by using referenda which have only the appearance of democracy.

It takes just a few people to destabilize a country. Armed struggle is within everyone's reach. Weapons can be bought on the open market. There is no lack of ideas, passions and group interests to stir up conflict. The terrorism in so many parts of the world shows that. Guerrillas show that as they bring entire states to their knees. In the 1970s, terrorist movements in Italy and Germany were set up and shook the country to its core. Today we can see how weak they were but in those days terrorism constituted a real nightmare for the people and the authorities (who in Italy does not remember the kidnapping of Aldo Moro by the Red Brigades?). Just a few people are able to destabilize the lives of many others.

Kareed Zakaria talks of the "democratization of violence". Violence, war and the use of fearsome weapons (including nuclear technology) are within reach of all people. I have often written of how today everyone can make war and execute their strategies of violence and terror. This is a conviction I have had for many years through contact with situations under the influence of rebel movements. Global as well as local terrorism expresses this predicament. Today it is easy for dissent which has no political and peace-making resources to turn to rebellion and armed struggle. Today women and men are significant and they can destabilize entire systems.

Take a brief look at the faces of our fellow human beings. In just a quarter of a century the inhabitants of the earth have changed. In 2006, for the first time in human history, the population of the cities exceeded that of the countryside.

Between 1980 and 2000 there has been a cultural revolution: the literacy rate of adults over 15 years of age has taken a great leap forward. This has important consequences for the relationship between individuals and the environment; the expectations of individual people are changing. In 1980, Chinese literacy was 66% of the population, today it is 85%. At the time of Khomeini's revolution in Iran 51% could read and write, in 2000 it was 77%. There have been spectacular developments in literacy: Nigeria has gone from 33% to 77%, Algeria from 40% to 63%, Rwanda from 40% to 67%, Afghanistan from 18% to 47%, Ivory Coast from 27% to 47%, Mali from 14% to 40%. It is estimated that, by 2010, adult literacy will reach 83% of the world population (in 1970, it was 63%). Emmanuel Todd has written, "Learning to read and write – not forgetting the elementary arithmetic that accompanies it – is only one stage in the mental revolution which has extended itself to every part of the planet."

The attitude of a literate person towards their own destiny is different from that of an illiterate. Aspirations change. Massive emigration in search of a better standard of living is revealing a mental revolution: people's horizons have been changed. This major culture-shift also links to an increased control of fertility. People are acquiring the capacity of looking beyond their own local and family environment and are putting themselves in touch with a larger world. They are locating themselves in an information loop, through which they know more or less what is happening and what life is like in other parts of the world. Women, differently in various cultures, are gaining a greater sense of their own individual destiny. Men and women feel that they are controlling their life more: yet the reality does not correspond to their aspirations and, at times, they are greatly disappointed. Rapid adaptation processes can tie them to unstable political phenomena as they seek to take their destiny into their own hands and aspire to democracy and fight against marginalization. This is happening today in many parts of the world.

The cultural revolution taking place is making women and men more aware of the value of their own lives. This awareness contrasts with the contempt for the life of individual people typical of the twentieth century. The century that saw the spreading of democracy was also a time of contempt for human life for the sake of achieving political ends, which were often totalitarian, their instigators proclaiming that they wanted to build a better tomorrow. According to Rudolf Rummel, violent homicides by governments in the twentieth century murdered almost 170 million human beings. This scholar calculates that there were almost 62 million victims during the seventy years of Soviet power. The Chinese Communists killed 35 million. We recall that during the "Great Leap Forward", the Maoist reform of the Chinese agricultural system, there were 27 million human beings who died of hunger. Such methods were in continuity with the mass murder practised by the Nationalist Government of Chiang Kai-Shek (more than 10 million deaths) and the Japanese military (6 million killed in the Second World War, of whom two thirds were Chinese).

The human sacrifice of enemies, were they "dissidents", opponents of the Communist project or any kind of citizen, was related to the achievement of scientific communist "truth". Society was being remoulded rapidly and obstacles had to be overcome. For Mao Zedong, the 600 millions of Chinese represented "a blank page". "A white sheet of paper" – he used to say – "has no marks on it and therefore the newest and most beautiful words can be written there..."

According to their differences in national culture and politics, the Soviets and the Chinese moved at high tempo to construct the new human being and the new society, overcoming structural and human obstacles. But the most insane expression of pure revolutionary society-building was Cambodia under the Khmer Rouge where more than 2 million people were assassinated in four years, 1975-9, and that does not take account of the hundreds of thousands who starved to death. This was the price for "a healthy and modern country during the 1990s", declared the leaders of Cambodia.

The twentieth century was the century of genocide and the criminal state, to take up Yves Ternon's phrase. Massacres were committed mainly by state authorities, who were sometimes profiting from wars. What emerges from all this is that even imperfect democracy is the best antidote to protect not only human rights, but life itself. Today, literate men and women have reached the end of a century which has stolen many human lives for the sake of utopian follies and they have become more conscious and jealous of the value of life. Respect for life is a boundary which no policy – national or international – can easily cross. This boundary takes effect in many ways: through the ordinary mechanisms of democracy, through valuing human rights, through a culture in which human life cannot be sacrificed for the sake of some project or other interest. Today the lives of the few and the little men and women in society cannot be brushed aside in the interests of the majority. This sense of boundary, becoming ever more deeply anchored in human consciences, constitutes a reference point for whoever is looking to the future of the world. There is much left yet to be developed, because this life-culture has barely been opened up to the lives of the "weak", whereas the "useful life" tends to be valued and may lead to eugenic practices or euthanasia.

The cultural revolution of the last decades cannot fail to have consequences on the way people look at the world. This is why I have said that we must look more intently into the faces of our contemporaries. These matter more than they did before. They know more things and they are looking for explanations about what is happening and about what they are seeing. What explanations will they find? During the 1990s, very many have made an emotional investment in national and religious identities to seek for answers: at a personal level they felt it necessary to identify with a larger reality. By following this road they have no longer developed a fascination with political ideologies but rather with nations and religions. Many political cultures certainly do exist, but nations and religions have offered many people the possibility of feeling part of a collective and having an identity in the world of globalization.

Many simplifications and counter-suggestions have arisen: this is only natural. But the fact remains that people possess literacy so that they can receive explanations and answers. One can say this much at least about Africa, a continent where millions of people have become participants in national pride but now live in a motivational void. There is a searching for motivations in the Muslim world. And in the United States, after the ending of the struggle against Communism, there is seen to be a need for a new sense of an appropriate "mission" in the world.

A new Christianity for the twenty-first century?

On the subject of the United States, many people in Europe have been surprised by the "religion" of the Americans. In the old continent, the Americans have been routinely considered to be the bearers of an emancipated vision of life: few have reflected on the religious roots of the American world. However, modernization has produced different results in Europe and North America. The United States have not been besieged by secularization as intensely as Europe. Still, a process of disaffection from the historic Churches has charac-

140

terized the religiosity of the American, beginning from the South in the nineteenth century, but these people have been leaving for communities with stronger personal participation.

Despite the separation between state and religion, the United States are – as G. K. Chesterton used to say: "a nation with the soul of a Church". One can see this in the "religious" conception of their role emerging from the speeches of the Presidents. Studying the American soul brings us into contact with an original matter, the vast neo-Evangelical world (about 70 million faithful in the USA) for whom the individual choice for conversion is decisive and whose book is the Bible. The individual American is a person of faith more through conversion than by tradition. The personal choice of religion is part of the process of reformulating one's own identity. The neo-Evangelical world is not only strong in the United States but has also spread into Latin America (where it is undermining the religious hegemony of the Catholics), into Asia (people speak of 70 million converts in China) and into Africa. In Brazil, as Cardinal Hummes has stated, Catholics made up 90% of the population in the 1970s; in 1991 they had become 83% and reached 2000 with 73%. Today they might be 67%, with a year on year fall of 1% in favour of the neo-Protestant movement.

In the space of a hundred years, neo-Protestants have gone from being a small group of believers to almost half a billion, at a speed unequalled in growth and numbers in the history of religions. African and Latin American governments are beginning to consider the electoral impact of what are called "sects" whose links with those in power are different from those of Catholicism. This new model of Christianity, a strong element on the American scene, does not cohere into one single ecclesiastical organization but is fragmented into many denominations and represents a formidable challenge to the historic Churches. It is giving a good answer for literate, individualized human beings because it insists on conversion and personal conviction and offers a sense of direction in a world where those human beings are feeling disorientated. It does this most of all through a welcoming environment which is often not found in the institutional Churches. Neo-Evangelicalism is located in a global American world-view, which is facilitating its spread, as, at one time, a colonial world-view favoured the historic Churches.

Yet the position of the Roman Catholic Church remains strong, as was shown by the general participation following the death of John Paul II. Uniquely international, Christian and close-knit (whereas the Orthodox Churches are autocephalous), the Catholic Church is strong in the United States. With its 62 million faithful, it is the biggest confessional body, although its influence is rather reduced because of the falling number of its faithful and the reduced strength of its institutions. At a world level, Catholicism on the one hand and Neo-Evangelicalism on the other now seem to be the principal currents in Christianity and in the religion of the West. However, we must not forget the historic Protestant Churches, despite their crises, nor Orthodoxy which is largely the faith of Eastern Europe and Russia. Catholicism has reaffirmed its religious identity: that was the message of John Paul II who distanced himself from the liberal relativism of European culture. Catholicism has preached the living together of different cultures and civilizations. On one side, it has absorbed different cultures (from Mexico to Africa and Asia); on the other, it has managed cohabitation with other cultures and religions. Yet it has not renounced communicating its own faith to the non-Christian world, and has modelled itself on the criteria of the various cultures. It has asked for religious liberty for all people; it has offered dialogue as the ground of encounter. This is a position in which the Orthodox and Protestants are also largely to be found. The

142

neo-Evangelical movement has a different attitude. It is more given to confrontation (especially in its missionary ethos), though these are not positions which tend towards unity. Such a movement as that does not carry within it the historic experience of the Church of Rome and its governing network. These two great Christian currents, one ancient as is the Catholic and the other young as is the neo-Evangelical have worked out two different (but not entirely divergent) visions of the world and of the community of believers within it.

Europe beyond the crisis

In matters of religion, Europe has generally chosen the way of separation. Some European states have a history of secularism, seen as emancipation from a confessional state. For Catholic states in particular, secularism is an important topic, as we have seen in recent debates on Christianity over the Constitution of the European Union. This is often linked to a vision of European states that belongs to yesterday. It is still open to discussion as to whether the European picture may have been deeply and ultimately changed by the traumatic events it has been through.

The crisis of Europe has a clear demographic component. According to some projections, the Europe of twenty-five states will have only 445 million inhabitants by 2050 and the only country to grow will be France, moving up from 61 to 65 millions. The crisis has political dimensions. The debate with the United States that has divided the Europeans during the war against Saddam Hussein still has about it the flavour of a family argument within a common focus, now more than half a century old. But what will Europe be like when facing new and strange negotiators such as the Asians?

The crisis of Belgium, a country which was at one time culturally important, gives us a clue, and the crisis in the Netherlands, which twenty-five years ago was open and permissive and ready to welcome other people along with their identities, is also significant in this respect. The European crisis manifests itself at various levels, but it seems to have a common anthropological background. Frank Furedi, a sociologist of Hungarian extraction, explains the growing fragility of our society on the dominance of emotions or, rather, on a "therapeutic vision" of life. Because of this we do not change nor does reality alter; we do not become better and we do not transcend ourselves; rather, we cultivate a powerful sense of personal vulnerability. A decisive feature of our times seizes upon this, a crisis in the model of masculinity which went through so many difficult phases in the twentieth century. This model (with its variants: the warrior, the militant politician, the entrepreneur, the conqueror) had a clear driving role in the history of our society. Today the situation is very different. This is no quick way of describing how our European crisis may have a clear anthropological underlying cause. There may be many difficulties in other societies but they are not the same crises (even in regard to a model of masculinity). Despite this, every European country carries within its history resources, potentialities and a secular heritage. Europe is still a resource for the entire world.

The European Union is becoming an answer to these questions. Although it does not suppress identities, it does allow a privileged rapport between countries and their image in the rest of the world. It can become a special area; not an empire but a connection of national destinies which are not only discovering they do not need to be in opposition to each other but that they are sharing a common future. This is an area without any national or political hegemony, brought about by a laborious convergence, slow and reactive, split by divisions

144

but at the same time something original in today's world. However, Europe needs to re-think itself from the roots upwards and do it before the eyes of the world. All we Europeans need a re-statement of our identity at a personal, collective and supranational level. We lack a sense of being European, as can be seen from the French and Dutch referenda and from other events. To create Europe, we need to appeal to the deepest roots and sentiments of its citizens. And, beyond the rhetoric, individual countries must make concrete choices.

The Europeans are going through an identity crisis which is also a spiritual one. Is not now the time for *ressourcement*, which means finding our own well-springs once again? During the Second World War a great secular philosopher, Benedetto Croce, recognized the role of Christianity in the history of Europe in an essay with the significant title, "Why we are unable not to call ourselves Christians". Croce considered Christianity to belong to the past rather than the present, yet still to be the basis of our culture. In some ways, secularism also plays its part in the cultural baggage of Europeans: for their part, Christians are unable not to call themselves secular. It is an aspect of our common inheritance which cannot be denied: it is not a dogma, it is a piece of history and a reality. What is more, the Second Vatican Council accepted and hoped for religious liberty. Today the debate on European identity has changed greatly. We cannot approach it with the categories of yesterday and omit consideration of fundamental secular motives and feelings over unity. It is something which we must take into account.

Our European world is secular and pluralistic, but it does have a special relationship with Christianity which is not only one of its historic roots but also the life-experience of millions of Europeans. In the debate on the European Constitution, I expressed my conviction that we should not be afraid of remembering Christianity. It was not understood that, for

145

Europe, this was the time for *ressourcement*. Affirming that this did not spring from a desire to unite Europe into one religious denomination, but from observing that there are gaps and from looking into Europe's deepest sense of direction. I also hold to my conviction that some clear reference should be made to Auschwitz, the low point, the infernal abyss of European history. It is from that point that Europe began its journey, when it took note of the evil of the war and the Shoah. A slow ascent from the abyss can be reckoned from 1945 onwards, when the world discovered that evil place, a monument to all the sorrows of Europe and to the most dramatic nationalistic madness of our continent. The recalling of Christianity would have spoken to the depths of the European mind.

We must have the courage to hold this debate on identity within a setting less marked by traditional national provincialism and its prejudices. Olivier Clément is a European able to listen deeply to Western culture and to Eastern sensibilities. He has written that there is a fundamental task to be done, "to draw together the spiritual that lies at the heart of European culture." And, utilizing an effective image, he adds, "If we do not want to return to the caveman, we must discover the human interior in the caverns within humanity itself." The great religious tradition of Europe remembers the spiritual dimension of humankind, for whom life itself is a mystery. This sense of the mysterious, through which the believer comes into contact with God, takes nothing away from liberty but rather affirms the deepest levels of human life, as the great theologian Henri de Lubac saw it, writing in the midst of the Second World War. In the course of European history, liberty has often been conceived as emancipation from the world of faith: the period of Illuminism, of the French and the liberal revolutions. It is also the history of European Socialism, deeply influenced by Marxism, but also by the desire for reform and by Utopianism. Finally, 1968 was like a European cultural revolution (the last to have pretensions to universality); in the name of liberation, it popularized revolutionary sentiment against authority and tradition. And what tradition is there in Europe that is stronger than the Christian? Nevertheless, this is a one-sided vision. The history of European Christianity is also a story of liberation. Consider only the twentieth century: the Second Vatican Council, the history of Christian movements which established democracy in Italy and in Germany, the Christian struggle against Communism in Eastern Europe... If we simply look at the evidence, the history of liberty in Europe still has important roots in Christianity. A Europe intent on rebirth must face up in a new way to this debate and to the interpenetration between society and spiritual issues, between its present reality and Christianity.

Realism and hope

Rabbi Jonathan Sacks has anxiously observed, "The absence of religious faith, added to the failure of the 'Illuminist Project' to create a universal ethic, results in moral relativism: a way of thinking (or rather a refusal to think) about life-choices which can be adapted to a consumerist culture but is totally inadequate in the defence of liberty when faced with a vehement, violent and fanatical challenge." The contemporary conscience is impoverished, pliable and defenceless when faced with movements or aggressive societies. Francis Fukuyama speaks of this phenomenon as "the great destruction" brought about by capitalism and consumerism: it is the using up of social capital, bonding and values. Sacks adds, "Relativism is not adequate to the challenge of ethnic assertiveness and exclusivist systems of belief." The men and women of our time are often defenceless when confronted by aggression or fanatical propaganda. The moral destruction of Western society – one thinks of crime in the United States or in the French banlieue – is generating violence from individuals who are finding an identity through aggressive behaviour.

Numerous alarms have been sounding over the presence of Muslims in Europe, especially after the attacks in London and the revolt in the banlieue. It is certainly not easy to manage the Muslim presence, because in some cases their communities are places where the culture is radicalism. But can we make war on the whole of Islam? We cannot send away immigrants who have become citizens of our countries just because they are Muslims. Oriana Fallaci does at least have the merit of consistency in her position of opposition to Islam in the name of the values of a Christian civilization (despite not sharing in the Christian faith). Her positions are clear: the basis for violence is in the Qur'an . Islam is the new Nazism. There are two choices, either the retreat to Munich by the Europeans faced with Hitler or the Second World War. Fallaci criticizes a "weak" interpretation of Christianity and calls for Europe to be nerved up in opposition to Islam. She proposes the exile of Muslim citizens from our countries.

I too, am convinced that our societies need to be defended, but we cannot – as I have already said – make the assumption that the whole of Islam carries a destructive message with it. The weakness of our societies lies in not knowing how to say – except somewhat confusedly – what our own identity might be, so as to allow for their integration or a pact to be made with them. "Enemy Islam" will not give us back our identity. This will only happen through a conscious process which calls for the courage to say who we are and to establish ourselves from a moral standpoint. This is a process entrusted to the freedom of individuals, to culture, to religious faiths. Christianity cannot be the banner under which Europe opposes Islam. It is so much more than that. The problem of the French suburbs is also characterized by the lack of relationships and shared values. As Régis Debray wrote, "Here the problem is not too much religion, but its scarcity." The conclusion is that the problem before us is the problem of speaking afresh to the human heart. Taking up religious traditions again answers this in part. The religions have a big task to perform. Islam has a large task in the training of its faithful and its leaders. But Christianity and Judaism also have the task not of pointing to an enemy, but of equipping individuals to live wisely and to live with other people.

Living with others demands relationships either of unfriendliness or of friendliness. The processes of unfriendliness often develop in the great emptinesses of our society today. The case of Dutch society, once so liberal, is evidence for this. So many religious identities (both Catholic and Protestant) have been eroded. Dutch Catholicism went to pieces after the 1970s. Today what remains is uncertainty, fear and aggressiveness. For Rabbi Sacks, globalization and emptiness of spirit are carrying us into "the greatest vulnerability" and we need to discover strong ideals within the scope of the great religious traditions which will allow us to live together, respectful of diversity, cultivating our faith and identity. Sacks emphasizes that the idea of a pact for living together comes from traditional religion. This is not to do with Abraham (the origin of the Jewish faith) but with a previous person, Noah. Such people acknowledge God as Creator and receive the commandment not to spill blood. In the light of this pact, we see a place for the differences in other people: "There is nothing relativistic in the idea of the dignity of difference."

The eminent Rabbi of Leghorn, Elia Benamozegh who died in 1900, put forward the idea of resuming the Noachian pact between the nations who were little cared for by Judaism and forgotten by Christianity. Such a pact is defined by the prophets of Israel as "an everlasting covenant" (Isaiah 24: 5). Its symbol is the rainbow which embraces every land and has become a symbol of peace in our own day. We read in Genesis 9 that the earth is mankind's responsibility. But human blood must not be spilt. It is a pact of respect and responsibility for one another: a Biblical Humanism open to all those who do not share the faith of Abraham. In Noah's pact it is written, "I will surely require a reckoning… from human beings, each one for the blood of another." (Gen. 9: 5) The first murder in the Biblical narrative is that of Abel by Cain, committed by a man who answered when asked where his brother Abel might be, "I do not know; am I my brother's keeper?" (Gen 4: 9) The pact with Noah declares that everyone will be asked to render an account for the life of the other person. The Biblical message is that whoever does not respect this pact brings violence into history and it will ultimately sweep them away. "Whoever sheds the blood of a human, by a human shall that person's blood be shed; for in his own image God made humankind." (Gen 9: 6)

How can the ancient pages of the Bible inspire such a pact in the present day with all its challenges and defiance? The great religions are able to educate people in living together through the concept of a pact. It is a pact with God; but it is also a pact between human beings to have respect and show responsibility towards one another. The pact is the art of holding differences together but it also brings sensitivity to the boundaries for which the other person stands. The pact is the basis for a shared culture which recognizes such differences. Revolutionary Utopianism suppresses any sensitivity to boundaries and behaviour codes of others: thousands and millions of people can therefore be killed to create a new world and a new kind of human being. The Utopianism of progress has lost any sensitivity to such boundaries. As the theologian Romano Guardini wrote, "The modern human being is of the opinion that every gain in power is simply progress; growth in security, usefulness, well-being, strength for living and full of value. In reality power is something polyvalent." The ideology of the market economy has lost it boundaries: the interests of the other person, of other groups or the general effect on everyone. The pact proposes respect for the boundary formed by the existence of the other person.

The civil practice of living together is not just a matter of the peaceful juxtaposition of communities, like some communitarian federation. Does not secularism, an integral part of the European heritage, bring with it the concept of a common destiny among different people, as if there were a secular pact? Secularism reminds us of a sense of statehood and the destiny of a national community. It is an affirmation of what we have in common. John XXIII used to teach that we must search for what unites and put aside what divides: this was his diplomatic and pastoral strategy. Community of interest creates something of a crossbreeding between the most diverse levels of life. Sixteenth century globalization brought this into being with the conquest of the Americas, producing the term "crossbreed" from the Latin *mixticius*, which means someone born of mixed race. It is a term also applied to animals to indicate their mixed origin and lack of purity. Crossbreed is a word which used not to exist in English or German. However, in Mexican culture, it is an expression of pride. The Mexican Virgilio Elizondo wrote of it with enthusiasm in a book The *Future is Crossbreeding* (using an expression of General de Gaulle's).

Even present-day globalization has created cross-breeding. This is not merely an ethnic matter but, most of all, something cultural. In the *Labyrinth of Solitude*, Octavio Paz wrote that the labyrinth of cross-breeding is ultimately "what is true for all human beings". Jacques Audinet adds lyrically, "History combines differences; history is cross-breeding and advances

151

only through what is cross-bred." Cross-breeding of cultures accompanies cross-breeding of people at times of emigration. The population of Rome is 7% foreigners and in 2003 there were 1,342 mixed marriages compared with 9,590 between Italians and 1,069 between foreigners. Almost one family in ten which came into being in 2003 is a cross-breed and their children will be "mixed".

On being asked why he, an African and a poet of *negritude*, had chosen to write in French, Senghor, the poet-president of Senegal, used to reply, "Because we are cultural crossbreeds; because, even though we feel that we are black, we express ourselves in French because French is a language which is naturally universal." Others who started from the same *negritude* would not have made that choice. Cross-breeding is a constant feature of ancestry and represents a choice to be connected with a plurality of cultures which demand that their inheritance shall come from a greater number of backgrounds. A cross-bred tapestry exists – at least from the cultural point of view – and it embraces all our various forms of human society. This is not one form of civilization having hegemony but of very many universal cultures which nevertheless have an infinite number of cross-breeding, superimposed in various areas and with multiple ancestries. This is the reality that is Europe within itself and in relation to other domains, such as the African one. How could Europe define its nature without referring to Russian culture (which belongs with us and differs from us at the same time)? And what criss-crossings of destinies and cultures took place in the United States in the twentieth century?! Behind rigidity of identity we so often discover cross-breeding, hybridization and creolization from histories both long and short.

Whatever else it may be, a Europe that is characterized by cultural strata and exchanges cannot be a continent of empty people. Spiritual and human roots do exist and a profound

152

shared identity is taking its direction from them. This identity is reformulated by voluntary choices but it also comes out of the history and geography that lies behind them. To a considerable extent, European nationalism itself has a spontaneous history which is not bound to ethnic determinism. In the European spiritual climate a strong sense of peace, reverence for life and valuing human life have now come to maturity.

Within this wide horizon of multiple ancestries, all people need to negotiate and develop a pact for living together. The cross-breeding that unites us suggests the need for this at every level; we must have a pact for living together with others who are not total strangers to us. Europe can play an important part in this process.

This Europe without any empire can, if it is strong in multinational solidarity, become a space of peace in the contemporary world. Its links with the United States and Latin America are clear. We have also spoken of Eurafrica. So many aspects of world cultures are in communication with our continent which rests upon both an ancient and a more recent cultural stratification. The Europe which is uniting itself is a space of peace inside a world where war has come back as an instrument for resolving conflicts. War renders the world more understandable as a picture in black and white. But it is a terrible mode of understanding.

There is no one single global solution in a world containing so many subjects, so many powers and so many forces – not even the solution produced by having one superpower, as the United States could be. We are accustomed to dealing with the question of the United States in the context of relations with Europe. But the emergence of the Asiatic world is putting the American empire into difficulty and creating new scenarios. Is there a political language common to the United States, the Asiatic world and China? Seen in perspective, this is a far more pertinent question than relations between Western countries and the Islamic world.

Deng Xiaoping, the constructor of the Chinese turn-around during times when China was hardly moving along the road of modernization, declared that his country refused all hegemony and was opting for a multi-polar picture in international relations. The prophecy attributed to Napoleon ("when China awakes the world will tremble") has already been fulfilled. Alain Peyrefitte, with his profound knowledge of Chinese society, wrote at the end of the twentieth century, "China has woken up." Yes, China has woken up and we are asking ourselves, "Shall we see a new cold war between the United States and China? Are those two countries competitors in the global economy or are they military enemies?" The Shanghai agreement between China, Russia and Muslim ex-Soviet countries seemed to be economic in character but successive Russo-Chinese military manoeuvres have revealed a background of strategic agreement which seeks to put limits on the presence of America. The reinforcing of relations between the United States and India (once an old Soviet ally) is opening the prospects for unannounced alignments and separations.

On the international scene, nothing is set in stone, but certainly confrontation with the Chinese giant, relations with the Indian giant and the problem of Pakistan's instability are topics which will be troubling American policy. And what of the small countries of Europe? On their own they can no longer do anything unless by concerted action, compromise and comparison with each other. India and China, on the other hand, are presenting as central realities in the near future, with their 2 billion and 300 million inhabitants, with their half a million engineers, computer specialists and diplomats (compared with the 60,000 trained in American universities, not all of whom are American), with their work force ready to undertake the most menial occupations and also the categories of their people with qualifications. It is forecast

154

that "Chindia" (China and India) will, within four decades, possess half of the production power on the planet.

How can we fail to understand, from now onwards, how we must face the reality of a multi-polar world? This is a world where every player knows that they cannot be a presence in each and every crisis; they must make agreements, collaborate, make use of others, create pacts and respect them. Even the strongest need other people. International politics must discover the reasonableness of a culture of living together. The European Union can be a powerful promoter of a similar vision, born of necessity in some areas, out of an interest in development or from the meeting of cultures. This is a dimension of international politics and of relations between civilizations and religions. In our time, no one body – not even the United States with their powerful industrial culture – can succeed in being truly global and universal. This means that everyone is needed, even the weakest. It is not only aggressive force that human groups – even small ones – can wield; all of us are necessary for dialogue and for relationships that involve the least powerful subjects. This is what I have tried to say in this book.

Utopian visions for the planet go from those far-off ideas of Christopher Columbus to those of modern management! These Utopias have had an illusory energy which has sometimes been violent. They are discredited by the complexities of the world and drawn into dialogue with an articulate view of the present time. When Utopias are discredited, it often produces a renunciation of any vision of a peaceful world. It causes people to resign themselves to the confounding of identities, to great aggressiveness in a difficult world and to the renunciation of any vision for the future. This is to accept that we almost live in the world like blind people, without knowing how to indicate the way ahead or offer ideals to the younger generation or give our own country a sense of direction. It is to accept only the task of protecting ourselves from unforeseen acts of aggression.

We are all different, and difficult to unify; however we are also united by very many cultural, political, financial and geographical connections, both positive and negative. The empires and the unification ideologies have disappeared. Distances have become shorter and people far away have been made neighbours through emigration. Old links are loosening and new ones being made. Giovagnoli wrote, "The globalized world... is not homogeneous and uniform dependence." In coming to know, in formulating alternatives, in connections, distances, proximities and cross-breeding, we are practising the art of living together, the fruit of realistic politics and human and religious hope. This is realism faced with a plural world. This is the hope that the madness of conflict will never be repeated. This is the realization of a civilization made up of many civilizations – if one may use that expression – or of very many cultural, religious and political universes. The awareness of the necessity of the civilization of living together is the beginning of a culture shared by different women and men. This culture is preparing the achievement of one or more pacts being made to live together and is already beginning to put the civilization of living together into practical effect.